King AI

KING AL

How Sharpton Took the Throne

Ron Howell

EMPIRE
STATE
EDITIONS

AN IMPRINT OF FORDHAM UNIVERSITY PRESS

NEW YORK   2021

Fordham University Press has no responsibility for the persistence or accuracy of URLs for external or third-party Internet websites referred to in this publication and does not guarantee that any content on such websites is, or will remain, accurate or appropriate.

Fordham University Press also publishes its books in a variety of electronic formats. Some content that appears in print may not be available in electronic books.

Visit us online at www.fordhampress.com/empire-state-editions.

Library of Congress Cataloging-in-Publication Data

Names: Howell, Ron, author.
Title: King Al : how Sharpton took the throne / Ron Howell.
Other titles: How Sharpton took the throne
Description: First edition. | New York : Empire State Editions, an imprint
    of Fordham University Press, 2021. | Includes bibliographical references
    and index.
Identifiers: LCCN 2021027085 | ISBN 9780823298877 (hardback) | ISBN
    9780823298884 (epub)
Subjects: LCSH: Sharpton, Al. | African American civil rights
    workers—Biography. | African American clergy—New York (State)—New
    York—Biography. | African American politicians—New York (State)—New
    York—Biography. | African American television journalists—Biography. |
    Clergy—New York (State)—New York—Biography. | Politicians—New York
    (State)—New York—Biography. | New York (N.Y.)—Biography.
Classification: LCC E185.97.S54 H69 2021 | DDC 973.92092 [B]—dc23
LC record available at https://lccn.loc.gov/2021027085

Printed in the United States of America

23 22 21   5 4 3 2 1

First edition

CONTENTS

King AI

INTRODUCTION

I WROTE THIS book in 2020, the year of America's reckoning with race—and a raging, deadly virus.

The wake-up moment on race arrived on May 25, 2020. Millions of stunned Americans stared at their screens, looking at the white cop in Minneapolis forcing his knee against the neck of a handcuffed Black man who was lying on the street, moaning that he couldn't breathe, calling out for his (dead) mother—all as the cop gazed at a camera recording the nine-and-a-half-minute murder. My memory will hold forever the phlegmatic, cold-blooded dismissiveness on the face of the cop.

Black young men and women around the country immediately began marching with newfound white allies, protesting loudly, demanding that the cop, Derek Chauvin, be charged with a capital crime for that murder seen around the world. (He was eventually charged with and convicted of second- and third-degree murder and manslaughter. As of this writing, that meant he was facing several decades in prison, as opposed to the life sentence many activists had wanted. Still, there was rejoicing around the nation for what was seen as an historic victory for racial justice.)

One person stood out for taking advantage of that singular 2020 opportunity to channel Black rage. And he was not a youngster. He was the sixty-six-year-old Al Sharpton, whose George Floyd eulogies, given in Minneapolis and in Houston, Texas (where Floyd was raised), went viral and solidified Sharpton's status as the country's longest-standing civil rights activist/leader. He led protests around the country, often with big-shot elected officials and with ministers affiliated with his politically influential National Action Network.

Most striking, in many ways, was that Sharpton did all he did in the midst of a once-in-a-century health crisis. The Covid pandemic killed hundreds of thousands of Americans and caused others to experience degrees of sometimes fatal angst. The U.S. Centers for Disease Control and Prevention reported on August 14, 2020, that that one out of four young adults answered "Yes" when asked if they had considered suicide in the past thirty days. Although it was later revealed that suicide among Americans overall declined through 2020, rates in Black and brown urban communities increased through the year (*New York Times*, April 19, 2021).

Through it all, Sharpton literally marched on. On one notable occasion, on August 28, 2020, he led an anti–police brutality protest in the nation's capital, exactly fifty-seven years after the historic "March on Washington," at which Martin Luther King Jr. gave his "I Have a Dream" speech. Mask-wearing was the rule at the event. Most news outlets reported that "thousands" were there with Sharpton. Sharpton, on *PoliticsNation*, said there were "200,000." (U.S. Capitol and Metropolitan D.C. police told me they don't offer numbers on such events.) For this book, I followed the advice of a Washington, D.C.–based television news cameraman who was at the march. He said to find photos and make my own call as to how many were there. He, like all reporters I spoke with, said he didn't have even a rough idea. I decided to compromise, writing in this book that "tens of thousands" were there with the Rev. that day.

Regarding the coronavirus, one "mainstream" newspaper stood out for beating up on Sharpton. That was the *New York Post*, which ran a

December 13, 2020, article with a teaser asking, "Why No Mask, Rev. Al?" The piece cited an unnamed resident who complained that Sharpton had not been wearing masks in an elevator. In true *Post* style, the headline said Sharpton "could be spreading more than the gospel . . ." at his Upper East Side condo development.

As this book will show, Sharpton has mastered the art of salvaging his reputation after credible complaints about his behavior. In March 2020, Rev. Horace Sheffield III of Detroit told the *Detroit News* that he came down with the coronavirus after being at a meeting with Sharpton and others at the National Action Network office in Harlem. This was before mask-wearing and social distancing had become ingrained in the minds of Black influencers, or, specifically, in the mind of Sharpton. I asked him recently about that. He sent me links showing how diligent he's been since that time. In November 2020, he launched the Choose Healthy Life Black Clergy Action Plan "to address COVID-19 and other health disparities in the Black community." In December, he and other Black ministers met with the nation's most trusted Covid expert, Dr. Anthony Fauci, and told Fauci of the need to pay more attention to the disproportionate impact of the virus on Blacks. With the PR acumen of old Madison Avenue, Sharpton announced at a February 25, 2021, press conference at Harlem Hospital that he had just received his first Covid vaccine (Pfizer) and called on wary Blacks to take theirs.

Sharpton told me in a March 6, 2021, text message, "Sheffield's testing positive and his subsequent hands-on work around coronavirus awareness was the impetus for me and others in the faith and civil rights community to prioritize this. We shifted from rhetoric on the pandemic to active hands-on involvement, because of the work of Horace Sheffield." I did not recall Sharpton's saying anything about Sheffield before my asking him.

The above-mentioned *New York Post* story suggesting Sharpton might be "spreading" the coronavirus was not abnormal for the way the paper dealt with the minister/activist/news host. The *Post*'s lexis regarding Sharpton contrasts sharply with its references to former President Donald Trump, whom they seem to be always defending. That's because of the paper's right-wing editorial bent.

Now, here's a confession (one of a few I'll make in this book): Despite my strong disagreements with the policies of the *Post*, it's often the paper I read first in the morning. I love my birth city of New York, and the *Post*'s local coverage is impressive, relative to that of the city's other dailies. It hurts me to say this, but the *Daily News* seems much weaker, with regard to the expanse of its reporting and the time it's able to invest in each story. Meaningful to me also is that during the Covid shutdown, when I was not having print editions delivered, I found the *Post*'s use of the PressReader app to be of standout quality. You click each page, and as the pages "turn," you tap and read the stories just as they appear in the print edition. It worked well on my iPhone and desktop computer. In contrast, I found that using the app to browse the *Daily News* did not produce a satisfactory result. Sometimes I would give up reading the *News*'s "e-paper," because the page images were inexplicably small, so small that I couldn't read them and I couldn't get help on the Internet or by phone.

This is all painful for me. Over the past ten years, I have written freelance opinion pieces for the *News*, complaining about gentrification and police brutality. The *Post* would not have welcomed those articles.

On February 25, 2021, the *New York Post*'s media writer, Keith J. Kelly, wrote that *Daily News* staffers are in a panic and supporters of the paper "are desperately searching for a local billionaire to save the 101-year-old tabloid." They were in mortal fear that the money-grubbing hedge fund company Alden Global Capital, an assassin of newsroom jobs, would take full control of Tribune Publishing, which owns the *Daily News*. As I write this, the near-term future of the

Daily News is in doubt. Many have expressed a belief that it will not survive much longer as a print publication. And there is a sense, in reading the *New York Post*, that *Post* owner Rupert Murdoch is taking delight in all this. (On May 21, 2021, Alden was in fact given the go-ahead to become owner of Tribune Publishing, thus controlling—and leaving in stronger doubt—the "future" of New York City's tabloid of the ages.)

The one thing, maybe the only thing, I'd say complimentary about Rupert Murdoch is that he stands out for the vigor with which he's challenged the dominance of social media outlets, which have been stealing revenue from newspapers. The most thieving and immoral of that bunch is Mark Zuckerberg and his information-sucking Facebook. Murdoch has been going after Facebook in Australia and around the world. It's about money and power.

The reality, of course, is that newspapers have been dying since the beginning of the twenty-first century. Among notable exceptions are the *New York Times* and two others that have billionaire owners. Those two are the *Washington Post*, owned by Jeff Bezos, and the *New York Post*, owned by Rupert Murdoch.

For many newspaper reporters, who always refer to their profession as their "craft," *King Al* may be a sad tale. That's because the book, in large part, is about the dying years of American newspapers, the end of the era when craft was king. Rising in its place were the cable news networks that drew more earnings and eyes, notable among them being MSNBC.

As an old-time journalist and observer of Black activism, I've marveled at Sharpton's longevity. He's still quoted, as he was decades ago, on all the racial crises of the moment. I must say that I've gulped a bit at his professional identity transformation. During 2020 and into 2021, I watched Sharpton just about every Saturday and Sunday evening, as he hosted MSNBC's *PoliticsNation*. I also viewed archived videos of the program.

Once, I was all but shocked to see that in June 2017 Sharpton interviewed a Mississippi elected official named Chokwe Lumumba.

I right away recalled the name Chokwe Lumumba from back in the 1980s, when I was a reporter for the *New York Daily News* and then for *Newsday*. At *Newsday* in 1988, I met with Lumumba and several friends of his, who were suspicious of Sharpton after the then-hustling young minister began trying to make connections with them. The following appeared in the October 21, 1988, edition of *Newsday*, in an article I wrote, quoting Lumumba:

> "Obviously we had to feel that a definite possibility existed he was working for the government, and we would have felt that way about him or anybody else who approached us in that manner," said Lumumba, an attorney and then-chairman of the New Afrikan People's Organization.

Wow, I thought, as I watched Sharpton's 2017 MSNBC segment. I knew Chokwe Lumumba had been mayor of Jackson, Mississippi, but I'd thought he was dead. Plus, this guy looked a lot younger than the Lumumba I knew.

Stupid, out-of-touch me. Sharpton's interviewee was, in fact, Chokwe Lumumba, but he was Chokwe Lumumba the thirty-four-year-old son of the man I knew. Junior had just been elected mayor of Jackson, Mississippi, the same city that his dad had been mayor of, until the senior Lumumba's sudden death in 2014, at the age of sixty-six.

The *PoliticsNation* segment with Lumumba the son began with Rev. Al's saying, "Joining me now from Jackson is Mayor-elect Chokwe Antar Lumumba. First of all, Chokwe, thank you for being on. And you know I knew your father well . . .".

In 2020, I asked Rev. Al about all that, and he said, "Chokwe [the deceased Black radical] and I became friends." Sharpton said he had helped Chokwe Lumumba through some difficulties as Lumumba struggled to hold on to political office.

From what I've learned, Sharpton's account makes sense—and is true to form.

Sharpton is a New Age activist-*cum*-newsman/wheeler-dealer politician whose evolution is told in the pages of this book.

Unquestionably, Sharpton had a role in the election of Joe Biden and Kamala Harris as, respectively, the new president and vice president of the United States. That was clearly why Harris, the first Black/Asian/female to occupy the second-highest office in the land, honored Sharpton with a one-on-one interview in which she spoke about Black History Month, the Covid virus, and the significant people in her political life. She also spoke about her background as a graduate of the historically Black Howard University and membership in one of the "Divine Nine," the revered reference to the Black sororities and fraternities that date back to the early 1900s—in Harris's case, the Alpha Kappa Alpha sorority, founded in 1908.

Sharpton's interview with Vice President Harris aired on *Politics-Nation* February 28, 2021.

1

Reverend Al and Me

WELCOME TO THE age of the new journalism, where the gathering and sharing of information overlap with political activism and promotion. The Rev. Al Sharpton occupies a top rung of that media hierarchy. His rise bested the bets of old-school newshounds, the guys (mostly white) who smoked cigarettes while they wrote articles for New York City newspapers, in the final years of journalism's Golden Age. No one from back in that time and place expected Rev. Al to be where he is today. His latest book is titled *Rise Up*, and in it he urges Americans to tackle the moral and ethical challenges confronting them in the age of Donald Trump. No other person on air in America confronted Trump with the consistency, directness, and effectiveness of Al Sharpton, who reaches millions of households each weekend with his MSNBC news show *PoliticsNation*. Add to that the hundreds of thousands of others he speaks to daily on his weekday radio broadcasts, syndicated via Radio One to fifty-six stations around the nation, including the most populated cities, east to west, north to south.

The story of the Rev. Al Sharpton is one of biblical proportions, of astounding transformation, of victory against generational odds. In the age of Donald Trump, Sharpton made many distressed Black

Americans proud, pointing his finger menacingly at the camera on each *PoliticsNation* show, into the virtual face of the racist-in-chief, as Sharpton's words flowed, improvised and strong—rarely mispronounced, as they had been on occasion back in his days of becoming.

Sharpton is a media icon to many Blacks, and over the past two years I have (sometimes with hesitancy) moved toward those legions.

I'll have to out myself here: Back in 1988, when I was a reporter at *New York Newsday* (Rest in Peace), I wrote the first of a number of stories I'd do about the Rev. Al Sharpton. That story quoted sources as saying Sharpton had worked with the FBI, in the early 1980s, to try to locate Assata Shakur. Born Joanne Chesimard, Shakur had once been on the FBI's Most Wanted list. A leader of the Black Liberation Army, she had been convicted of and imprisoned for the 1973 killing of a New Jersey State trooper, Werner Foerster. But then, in 1979, comrades engineered her escape from prison. It was one of the boldest escapades in American history. Shakur's whereabouts had remained unknown, to the public, until Les Payne, a top editor at *Newsday* (and a founder of the National Association of Black Journalists), in 1987 got word that Shakur was in Cuba, under a grant of asylum from Fidel Castro, and he selected a journalist to go interview her in Cuba. Les chose me, because of my fluency in Spanish and because he knew I could relate to Shakur.

I spent a week with Shakur traveling around Havana and interviewing her at her home and other locations. I came back to New York and wrote an exclusive front-page story "On the Run with Assata Shakur" that was picked up by news outlets around the country. Speaking to me after the article ran, FBI official Ken Walton told me that he "or somebody like [him]" would one day capture Shakur and bring her back to the United States to stand trial.

Then, a year after the article was published, several Black radical activists met with me and laid bare their experiences with Al Sharpton in the early 1980s. They said he was trying to get them to open up about their friendships with Shakur. They resisted Sharpton's outreaches and said they were glad they had done so. Their concerns, they believed, were legitimized by a New York *Newsday* series of stories that appeared in January 1988. The investigative team of reporters revealed that Sharpton had been working behind the scenes with federal investigators, as part of a 1983 agreement with them. The Black radicals told me they believed Sharpton was, in fact, trying to obtain information about Shakur and turn it over to the FBI.

My October 21, 1988, article about the meeting with those Black radicals was on page 1, with the headline "The Minister and the Fugitive." Sharpton and his associates responded with anger. Over the years, they questioned my professionalism and integrity. In 1991, Michael Klein wrote an authorized biography of Sharpton titled *The Man Behind the Sound Bite: The Real Story of the Rev. Al Sharpton*, and in it he cast doubt on the existence of the "unnamed 'law enforcement' source" I cited in my article about Rev. Al and Assata Shakur. (The FBI source, speaking off the record, told me that, yes, Sharpton was supposed to be working for them, and, yes, one of his missions was supposed to be to locate Shakur.) I feel free now to name that source, given that he died in 2018. He was John Pritchard. Pritchard was Black and had worked in the 1970s and '80s to entrap and secretly record Mafia kingpins and soldiers, as well as Black radicals.

But I'll add this: Regarding Sharpton's supposed efforts to help catch Assata Shakur and other Black revolutionaries, I have discarded the hardened resentment that dominated me as recently as several years ago. I offer the following: Pritchard, the former FBI agent who was my law-enforcement source, said in his 1988 conversation with me, that while Sharpton was supposed to be gathering information for the Feds about Assata, he (Pritchard) had no idea whether Sharpton was actually trying to learn Shakur's whereabouts—or whether he was just pretending. I had sources, former Black revolutionaries, who were certain Rev. Al was trying to get them to tell him where Assata was. Those working for white New York City newspapers three decades ago, including Black me, had a running fest with that episode in Sharpton's life.

Among us in society today are a number of aging Black radicals who remain distrustful of the Rev. because of his past work with the Feds. They are largely quiet, perhaps fearing Sharpton's current influence. At least one of them, Ahmed Obafemi, who had been an ally of Assata Shakur's and a source for two articles I wrote about Sharpton and Assata, has been in a nursing home in Atlanta, Georgia. He told me in a phone conversation in 2020 that his opinions about the Reverend haven't changed an iota. "He's a con man," he said.

Sharpton's character and personality can be subjects for another book. But I assert here that over the past three decades his behavior patterns have changed to his credit and to the credit of Black people. Sharpton lets his anger about America's enduring slave past come out in just about everything he says. And, yes, he says a lot. His ability to speak off-the-cuff, and at length, with streaming, quotable turns-of-phrases makes him beloved, especially to Christian churchgoing Blacks. It is that last group that makes Al Sharpton so politically powerful.

Sharpton's righteous fuming was especially audible in the age of Donald Trump. He railed against Trump weekly on *PoliticsNation*. In August 2020, he organized a "Get Your Knee Off Our Necks" rally attended by tens of thousands of mask-wearing Blacks and whites in Washington, D.C., right near the White House. Sharpton had shown his power and influence also during the two presidential terms of Barack Obama, acting as an official stand-in for Obama, defending the nation's first Black president against attackers white and Black (like the Black scholar and Harvard professor Cornel West, who bashed Obama for not doing enough for struggling Blacks).

For me—and for other journalists who covered Rev. Al in New York in the last decades of the twentieth century—what stands out most is that Rev. Al is today, by measures used in our post-newspaper society, a journalist. What's more, he has a wider audience than any of the tabloid reporters who trailed him around New York. And he makes much more money than they ever did, many millions of dollars in wealth accumulated over recent years from cable salaries, radio-generated income, royalties from the books he's written (he says *Rise Up*, published by Hanover Square, sold 10,000 copies in the first week of distribution), income as leader of his nonprofit National Action Network, and payments from non–civil rights speaking engagements handled by booking agencies. And, unlike many reporters who covered Sharpton's noisy press conferences back in the day, Sharpton is alive—his physical survival attributable to exercising and dieting, which have enabled him to shed more than half the 300 pounds he once carried.

Ernest Tollerson was a journalist at New York *Newsday* and later at the *New York Times* over the last two decades of the twentieth century. At *Newsday*, he was the editorial page editor and edited commentaries about the young Al Sharpton shuffling from one controversy to another, most notably—to most readers—the Tawana Brawley episode. Tollerson, who is Black, told me: "Al Sharpton's recovery from the Brawley scandal and his ability to become a leading opponent of police brutality in New York City and, as time passed, everywhere in the United States is an incredible story, none of which is well understood here in New York City, the region, or in the nation at large . . . ." (Tollerson in recent years has been doing volunteer work with nonprofit organizations in New York State.) In a note to me, he said he was honored to have been able to witness, from a virtual front-row seat, the late-twentieth-century acts in the Shakespearean drama of Al Sharpton.

Sharpton's victories in life did not come just because he was in the right places at the right times. Sharpton's triumphs developed, in good part, from his early introduction to Black Christianity, specifically to Pentecostalism, which, perhaps more than anything else, set him on the path to what would be a gripping chapter in Black history.

There is a genius in Al Sharpton that has not been typically recognized in profiles of him written by journalists over the years.

"Brother Sharpton is a unique figure in American history, a figure who brings together so many different elements," said Cornel West, former Harvard Divinity School (but as of July 2021 Union Theological Seminary) scholar of politics and theology, speaking to me in the fall of 2020. "He has unbelievable energy and vitality and consistency in regard to being there at all the critical times."

As for the crises and controversies Sharpton faced (and often caused) a generation back in New York City, West added, "No one would have thought, going back to the '80s, that he would ascend to the heights where he is today."

West had battled bitterly with Sharpton, especially over West's strong criticisms of President Barack Obama for not, in West's determination, being radical enough in coming up with programs and statements benefiting Black communities.

Sharpton, said West, "is a combination of the power brokers coming out of New York, and on a national level he comes out of a very deep prophetic church tradition. . . ."

What is almost always left out of commentaries about Sharpton, West said, is his seemingly inborn brain power. "One thing overlooked is just the sheer power of his intelligence. People don't accent that enough, but he's got it."

Once derided as the most unscholarly New Yorker in the public sphere, Al Sharpton is today organizing a group of highly respected academicians who are backing his planned Museum of Civil Rights, to be located on West 145th Street in Harlem. Among those on the board of Sharpton's Civil Rights Foundation is Father Joseph M. McShane, president of Fordham University, which oversees Fordham University Press, publisher of this book. (Disclosure: Until late January 2021, I had no idea of Father McShane's connection.)

Sharpton says the Museum will cost $50 million, of which $5 million has been raised, and will open in 2024, displaying the intersectional struggles of Blacks, Latinos, women, and gays. Hearing tidbits like this about Al Sharpton makes old-time newspaper reporters fall silent in momentary disbelief. Among the words likely to finally escape are ones they would utter on deadline, when they had a great story: You can't make this shit up.

Seen Through History

Rev. Al's legacy is a testament to an endurance and boldness steeped in Black American history. It recalls the former Black slaves who in the mid-1800s pulled their shoulders back and became members of the U.S. Congress and business leaders. But Sharpton's is also a story of Black Brooklyn.

Sharpton's family came from the American South to Brooklyn during the bustling years of the Great Migration. He and I share that birthplace and that time, Black Boomers from Black Brooklyn, though I am several years older; I was born in 1949, he in 1954.

Sharpton's mom and dad had migrated to Brooklyn, respectively from Alabama and Florida; and Sharpton struggled through heavy hardships during his childhood years. My families on both sides came from the old British Caribbean, and my life was relatively privileged. But as we've shared thoughts a bit over the past two years, we've noted that we carry an inner devotion to that place, Brooklyn, that was a blending of traditions from the Western Hemispheric region of the African diaspora.

For a valued perspective, I reached out to a long-forgotten political pioneer from that old place in time, Waldaba Stewart. Stewart, who had immigrated from Panama in the early 1960s, entered local politics in the late 1960s. The reigning political boss of Brooklyn—mob-connected Meade Esposito—hated Stewart and took delight in telling journalists that Stewart's first name, spelled backward, was "a bad law." But Stewart was elected to the state senate in 1968 and made a mark. Speaking with me in 2020, he recalled being at an event, in about 1969, where a teenager named Alfred Sharpton appeared and spoke to a gathering at a church in the poverty-stricken neighborhood of Brownsville. Stewart was stunned at the young man's ease with words and remembers the speaking talent that stuck in his memory. Stewart left electoral politics in 1972 to become a college teacher (at Medgar Evers College) and an activist with the International Methodist Church. Living now in solitude in Manhattan (his beloved spouse, Esmeralda Brown Stewart, having died in 2019), the mid-octogenarian Stewart sees Sharpton sitting on a pedestal.

"There's no Black in America now who's more significant than he is," Stewart said of Sharpton. "Some question things he's done in the past, but those are mistakes that so many, the best and most well intentioned, make; and the important thing is keeping our character sincere and being upright. He stood next to Barack Obama during Obama's time in office and he [Sharpton] rose from the ground levels of Brooklyn to the highest seats in the United States of America."

2

Les Payne Sounds the "Death Knell" on the Tawana Brawley Story

SCHOLARS OFTEN REFER to American journalism's Golden Age as the period from the late 1800s to the beginning of the 1900s. That was when Ida Tarbell exposed the evils of industrialism with her classic investigative work published in *McClure's* magazine. Her model of long-form investigative reporting saw lasting impact as a book, *The Standard Oil Company*. During that era, her colleagues, the so-called muckrakers, wrote about and shot photographs of those living through poverty in America, notably New York City.

Some journalism historians have maintained that the Golden Age existed in stages, the last one stretching over the final decades of the twentieth century, from the 1970s to 2000. That last phase would be from the reporting on the Watergate scandal of the early '70s to the final decade when the Internet entered the ego of mass communications. The journalists from that last phase wrote the first drafts of the history that made us who we are.

In New York City, those last years were a stage, and onto it, in the early 1980s, stepped a young Rev. Al Sharpton.

The newspaper world then, in New York and beyond, was white (and male). But some courageous Black journalists were beginning to assert themselves. In the 1980s, no one in the New York region commanded more respect, from Black readers and fellow journalists, than Les Payne.

Payne was climbing the ladder of influence at the highly respected Long Island, New York, tabloid, *Newsday*. In 1985, *Newsday* made the gallant move of starting a New York City edition, called *New York Newsday*. Unfortunately for the Black residents of New York City, Payne was not based in New York City but rather in Suffolk County, Long Island, the home of *Newsday*. Suffolk County at that time was heavily white, clustered with racially segregated towns and villages. Payne in the 1960s would write about the racism he and his wife, Vi Payne, experienced trying to buy a home for themselves and their three children. The Paynes eventually settled into a beautiful detached house with a spacious yard in Huntington, in northwestern Suffolk County.

The white families on Long Island, composed of Suffolk County and its neighboring Nassau County, were largely white ethnics of Irish, Italian, and Jewish descent who had begun abandoning the increasingly Black New York City boroughs of Brooklyn and neighboring Queens from the 1950s through the 1970s.

Al Sharpton was one whom whites feared and wanted to keep at a distance. Even before Sharpton became a big name, white Long Islanders easily picked sides in New York City racial conflicts. Many *Newsday* readers wrote letters-to-the-editor saying they very much identified with a New Yorker whom both Sharpton and Les Payne (in his widely read columns) were militantly denouncing.

That was Bernhard Goetz, a tech geek who was riding the subway in Manhattan on December 22, 1984. He reacted spontaneously when four Black teenage males approached him in a Manhattan subway car. One of them asked Goetz for $5.00, and he responded, saying, "I have $5.00 for each of you" and pulled out an unlicensed .38 caliber revolver, shooting the four, leaving nineteen-year-old Darrell Cabey paralyzed for life.

New York City mainstream newspaper reporters did not know Al Sharpton. His life theretofore had largely been under the surface, with Brooklyn politicians, some of them so shady they wound up indicted or imprisoned, and also with Black, Italian, and Jewish American hustlers in the music industry. But Sharpton was starting to rise up beyond his roots, and he extended his still-existing "boy preacher" voice to the ears of media outlets that would listen, confined as they were for him at that point.

The *New York Amsterdam News*, a Black weekly newspaper, reported in February 1985 that Sharpton and Brooklyn activist minister Rev. Herbert Daughtry had met with U.S. Attorney Rudolph Giuliani. They told Giuliani that the federal government should step in because the local prosecutorial system was too racist to give justice to the Black shooting victims.

Reacting to a Manhattan grand jury's decision not to indict Goetz, Sharpton issued a statement saying, "This is a blatant slap in the face . . . to Black people. To say that a man with three guns, with dum dum bullets who said he shot until he ran out of bullets . . . to say he operated in self-defense in light of all this is abominable to anyone with common sense." Sharpton was whetting the rhetorical knives that would become sharper over the decades.

But in those days it was Les Payne who epitomized the skillful application of language in attacking racial violence.

In his columns, Payne referred to "Bernie" Goetz as the "blond haired, blue-eyed gunman." New York City Mayor Ed Koch thought Payne was going overboard with his columns and said so in a bitter reaction published in *Newsday*. At the time of the Goetz episode, I was just starting out at *New York Newsday*, having decided to leave Mexico City, where I and my wife and son had been living for the previous two years. I had been working with the Associated Press there.

I was so heartened by the forcefulness of Payne's columns on Goetz that I thought I might be able to stay at *Newsday* comfortably for a stretch of time. I'd previously been bouncing around. At that moment, I was in my early thirties, and already I'd worked for the

New York Daily News, the *Baltimore Evening Sun*, *Ebony* magazine, and the Associated Press. Maybe now, I thought, I could settle down for a decade or so.

"Tell the truth, then duck" was the way Les Payne described the job of a journalist, especially a columnist. The reaction against Payne by many whites on Long Island, especially police officers, was sometimes fierce. He received threatening letters, making *Newsday* realize they had to monitor his safety. Once, someone sent *Newsday* an image of Payne's face as a target on a Long Island police firing range. *Newsday* alerted its security operation.

As the next few years spun before us, Payne began to watch with puzzlement as Al Sharpton garnered increasing attention, appearing on the front pages of all the New York City daily newspapers: the *New York Daily News*, *New York Newsday*, and the *New York Post*. The focus on Sharpton really picked up in 1986 and 1987, as he joined an already-existing cohort of Black ministers, activists, and attorneys challenging patterns of violence against Blacks, especially young men. This intensified after a December 20, 1986, incident in the Howard Beach section of Queens. That was when a white mob attacked twenty-three-year-old Michael Griffith and two other Black men after their car had broken down. The white men chased Griffith onto a nearby parkway where he was struck and killed by a passing vehicle.

Then, in late November 1987, there came the news that a fifteen-year-old Black youngster from Wappingers Falls, New York, was saying that four white men had raped her. That was the beginning of the Tawana Brawley story.

Sharpton began partnering with two lawyers, C. Vernon Mason and Alton Maddox, holding press conferences demanding justice for the teenager, saying she'd been held against her will, raped, and covered with feces by a group of white men in Dutchess County, New York. Some of the allegations seemed beyond bizarre. Sharpton at one point declared that the Irish Republican Army was involved. The Brawley advisers began saying that a Dutchess County prosecutor, Steven Pagones, was one of the attackers. No story had shaken the city and region as disturbingly as Tawana Brawley's. This was the thick of the New York City tabloid wars. Blood was gushing daily, as life-sustaining printer's ink into the arms of New York newspapers.

Because of his high-ranking status at *Newsday*, Payne had to focus much of his attention on hiring, and on the assigning of stories to national and foreign correspondents. He also dealt with bitter in-house rivalries common in big companies—yes, even those in the mission of "truth-seeking."

Given the racial import of the breaking Brawley story, Payne's thoughts began to transcend internal political machinations at *Newsday*. He saw Brawley's as a Black story, one of the biggest to break in the New York region since he began working at *Newsday* in the late 1960s. And even though he was a top editor and columnist—and not a reporter—he wanted to be in on the making of the story, from the ground.

Like Sharpton, Payne had roots in Alabama. Payne's connection to Alabama was actually deeper than Rev. Al's. While Sharpton was born in Brooklyn to an Alabama mother, Payne saw his first light in Tuscaloosa, Alabama, and he was raised there during the Jim Crow era of the 1940s. Payne was more than ten years older than Sharpton and, as a boy, had worked picking cotton in Alabama fields. He later migrated to Connecticut, living there with his mother before attending the University of Connecticut, where he was in the ROTC (Reserve Officers' Training Corps). He became an Army Ranger, going off to Vietnam as a captain. He served in public information, under General William Westmoreland. For all his military background, Payne displayed a Black militancy that showed itself in his comportment at *Newsday*, as he battled for more respectful treatment of Black employees and helped found the National Association of Black Journalists.

Payne began to feel that Blacks across the region were being let down by a spreading of falsehoods in the Brawley matter. In October 1988 a state grand jury issued a 170-page report concluding that Brawley had not been kidnapped or sexually assaulted. There was no explanation of exactly what had happened.

Payne felt that reporters "on the ground" were not handling the Brawley story as they should have been. He found a kindred soul in the upper ranks of *Newsday*. That partner was Peter Eisner, with whom Payne had developed a close relationship. Eisner was *Newsday*'s Foreign Editor and reported to Payne, who was the paper's Assistant Managing Editor for Foreign and National News.

Eisner told Payne that he (Eisner) had police sources up in Dutchess County, from Eisner's earlier years working at the *Poughkeepsie Journal*. (Poughkeepsie is the county seat of Dutchess County.)

One day, Payne and Eisner traveled up to Poughkeepsie to see what they could learn. Eisner recalls that he reached out to some people he knew while Payne energetically began using sources that he himself was developing, making one call after another, pumping them for what they would offer in the way of information about the Brawleys. That part of the reporting craft had seeped into Payne's personality during the early 1970s, when he traveled as a reporter for *Newsday*, tracing the flow of heroin through the "Golden Triangle" of Asian countries into Corsica, the island in the Mediterranean, where the Italian Mafia dominated. Payne and his investigative team wrote a series of articles titled "The Heroin Trail," which won the 1974 Pulitzer Prize for Public Service and became a book.

In his reporting on Tawana Brawley, Payne ultimately came up with a story that took the mask off of what had happened up there in Dutchess County two years before.

After he got back to the *Newsday* newsroom in Melville, Long Island, Payne wrote an article that was based on interviews with Daryl Rodriguez. Rodriguez was a former boyfriend of Tawana Brawley, the teen who Sharpton, Maddox, and Mason asserted was raped by a group of white law-enforcement officers. Rodriguez opened up with Payne and said Tawana had told him she made up the tale because she was afraid of her mother's "significant other," Ralph King, who she feared would abuse her if she didn't have an excuse for not being home during that time frame in November 1987. King had served time in prison for stabbing and killing his previous partner.

"Tawana Brawley has confided to a friend that she and her mother faked the widely publicized rape and racial assault to prevent Ralph King, her mother's live-in love, from punishing the teenager, the friend has told *Newsday*," Payne wrote in his *Newsday* story.

According to Payne, Rodriguez, Tawana's ex-boyfriend, opened up about the incident because he had become frustrated and morally conflicted about all that had resulted from what was being called a "hoax."

"She just told me what I needed to know to clear my mind," Rodriguez told Payne. "She just thought she would tell me this because I had a right to know. And that's about it. Her parents, they messed up. They messed up."

Payne's article made the front page and totaled five full pages, with photos. It was headlined "Tawana Made It Up" and ran in the April 27, 1989, editions of the New York and Long Island newspapers.

(I was one of the contributing reporters on the article, having traveled to Virginia at Payne's request to get reactions from Tawana and Ralph King, who denied there was any truth to the report. Tawana and the whole family continued, from then on, to say their initial allegations were true. Even Sharpton began backing off the assertions. To this day, however, including in 2020 conversations with me, he maintains there is no firm proof that the Brawley story was made up.)

Clem Richardson, a former *New York Newsday* reporter who covered the Brawley story, said in a conversation with me in the summer of 2020 that Les Payne's scoop was the "death knell" for the Brawley saga. "Les was probably the most revered Black columnist at the time," Richardson said.

Payne and *Newsday* experienced immediate blow-back from Sharpton and his associates. The very day the story ran in *Newsday*, it was picked up by news agencies and widely spread on radio and television. The Sharpton team lashed out at Payne. On April 28, a *Newsday* story bearing Clem Richardson's byline reported that the Sharpton crew was saying that the Payne article was part of a "personal vendetta" by Payne against Sharpton. A Black newspaper based in Brooklyn, *Big Red*, ran a front-page commentary that encapsulated the reaction of many in the Black community. In blaring type at the very top of the front page screamed the headline: "Just a Payne in the Butt." (*Big Red* over the years became subsumed into the *New York Beacon*, which still exists.)

Payne, ever the soldier, agreed after his Brawley story to be a panelist for an event at Bed-Stuy's Slave Theater, where Sharpton and the Brawley lawyers held community meetings. He withstood a suggestion that he, as a former high-ranking U.S. army officer, might have had the interests of the federal government in mind more than the interest of Black people, in writing his Brawley exposé. All but shrugging, he calmly said that in the 1960s he was just a Black kid who got a chance to attend a respected college and fulfill his draft obligation by joining the ROTC. No one else followed up on the suggestion he was working against the Black community. His past working for Blacks in and out of the journalism profession was known around New York and the country.

Even so, according to Pamela Newkirk, in her book *Within the Veil: Black Journalists, White Media* (New York University Press, 2000), Payne "became the target of black talk-radio venom" and on WLIB there was "furious reaction from black callers and in-studio guests, including Sharpton" who said, "You have to be an imbecile, an idiot or a fool, or a reasonable combination of all three, to believe" what Payne had written.

As do many of the journalists from those days in New York, Clem Richardson expresses amazement at Sharpton's rise in popularity and power in the twenty-first century. He dethroned the kings.

"That's the wildest part, that he's a top cable television news host," Richardson added.

Others Join Payne in Voicing Doubts

If Payne landed the breaking news blow that took the Brawley crew down, other journalists also had significant roles in the ultimate determination by most Americans that the rape did not happen.

Two books were written by journalists who toiled in the vineyard of Poughkeepsie covering the Brawley story. One was *Outrage: The Story Behind the Tawana Brawley Hoax*, published in 1990 by Bantam Books and written by several staffers of the *New York Times*. That effort seemed motivated by a determination to once and for all close the book, as it were, on the case. Oddly, the strongest piece of evidence the book used to conclude that the Brawley story was indeed a "hoax" was toward the end of the 404-page volume. It was there that the writers presented readers with the words of the young man who, more than anyone else, showed that Tawana Brawley had colluded with her mother, Glenda Brawley, and Glenda's boyfriend, Ralph King, to dupe the public. That source was none other than Daryl Rodriguez, the very one who had been the source for Les Payne's exclusive *Newsday* article in 1989.

It was stunning and, to some Black journalists, unethical to use Payne's source without giving him credit for breaking that critical part of the overall story. Even before the publication of the book, Payne harbored anger, a feeling that the *New York Times* had all along been downplaying his work. He belittled *Times* reporters in a *Newsday* column. And in August 1989, when the National Association of Black Journalists held its annual convention at the Hilton Hotel in New York City, Payne was notably upset that there had been a panel on the Tawana Brawley story—and that he was not one of the scheduled participants. (He blamed the influence of the *Times* for that.) With chin out, lids halfway down his eyes, in his menacing manner, Payne grabbed a chair and, with everyone in the hall watching, marched toward the stage, climbed up to it, and placed a seat among the other panelists, joining them in an exchange about Tawana Brawley.

(One of the Black reporters on the Brawley story for the *New York Times* was E. R. Shipp. Shipp was also among the credited authors of the *Times* book. She eventually left the *Times*, complaining about her treatment there. She moved over to the *New York Daily News*, where in 1996 she won a Pulitzer Prize for commentary. Shipp is currently a professor at Morgan State University.)

The *New York Times* book account was preceded by another book outlining the dramas of the Brawley case—*Unholy Alliances: Working the Tawana Brawley Story*, by Mike Taibbi and Anna Sims-Phillips. It was published by Harcourt in 1989. Taibbi and Sims-Phillips had covered the story for WCBS-TV News.

Payne survived the onslaught from those angered by his article and may have even enjoyed much of it. Payne went on to oversee *Newsday*'s coverage of George H. W. Bush's 1991 war in Iraq, sending me to be part of a team that reported out of Saudi Arabia, Kuwait, and Iraq. Payne stayed with the paper as a top editor until his retirement in 2006. He died suddenly of a heart attack in 2018.

Two years after his death, Payne's long-researched book *The Dead Are Arising: The Life of Malcolm X* (Liveright) was published to rave reviews. The book was completed by Payne's daughter Tamara ("Tami") Payne. The biography of the assassinated Black nationalist Malcolm X is being praised for the depth of the twenty-eight years of research that Payne put into it, and also for the quality of the writing.

In the book, Payne offers touching details about the abuses and pains that caused the Great Migration of Blacks from the South in the

1940s and '50s. In that sense, it offers insights into the backgrounds of other Black history-makers, including Payne himself and the Rev. Al Sharpton.

He tells the story, for example, of a 1950s Connecticut admirer of Malcolm X. Her name was Rosalie Glover, and she had left Quincy, Florida, for Hartford in 1941. Sharpton's father was from Florida (though his mom was from Alabama, as Payne was).

Rosalie Glover had left Florida after whites had attacked and killed a Black man she knew there. Payne writes in the book that no local news outlet had reported on the killing of that man, A. C. Williams. Payne goes on to report that one American newspaper, the *New York Post*, stood out for exposing details about the killings of southern Blacks like A. C. Williams. The *Post* was "one of the few mainstream newspapers that paid attention to human rights violations against Negroes in the South in the 1940s," he writes.

Dorothy Schiff had purchased the (then) liberal *New York Post* in 1939. In 1976, Rupert Murdoch bought it, and the *Post* became known for its strongly right-wing approaches to issues and stories relating to Blacks. This was true through the rise of Al Sharpton. In the thick of Sharpton's late-1980s protests and soundbites, the *New York Post* stood out for its treatment of that phase as a kind of *Amos 'n' Andy* show. The *Post* was known not so much for the Tawana Brawley stories it broke but for a front-page photo and accompanying article it ran in 1988, of Sharpton sitting under a hair dryer at a beauty parlor that he regularly went to.

On November 18, *The Dead Are Arising* won the prestigious National Book Award for nonfiction. "[T]his intensely human portrait is written with a dedicated beauty and uncompromising detail that matches Malcolm's own life," the National Book Foundation said.

About a year before his death, three years before the publication of *The Dead Are Arising*, Payne and his family ran into Rev. Sharpton at a gathering. The then-retired journalist Les Payne and the TV news host Al Sharpton greeted each other warmly, like old friends, with Payne's daughter Tami snapping a photo of the two of them smiling genuinely.

On June 11, 2021, *The Dead Are Arising* won journalism's highest honor, the Pulitzer Prize, for biography.

Payne stood out for making a lasting, final impression on the Brawley story. But a lesser-known writer for a lesser-known publication also had an impact. The writer was Philip Nobile, and the publication was a music magazine called *Spin*.

Rev. Al Sharpton lived the '70s, '80s, and '90s on stages next to the biggest rock and soul stars of the era, most notably James Brown and Michael Jackson. He worked for them, promoted them. They were almost there, invisibly in the background, as Sharpton spoke on public stages, bellowing flowing, rhythmic phrases, as he spoke on the streets, or at press conferences, or in one-on-one interviews with writers.

That need to perform must have explained why Sharpton sat down for an extended interview with freelance writer Philip Nobile, who was writing an article for the February 1989 issue of *Spin*, which was a music lover's alternative to *Rolling Stone*. Among other stories, that issue of *Spin* contained an engaging piece about pop star Roy Orbison, who had just died in December 1988. The headline on the profile of Sharpton should have told him, if he didn't already know, that it was meant to sting him. It was: "Bonfire of the Inanities."

In the article, Sharpton laid out for Nobile the meticulous details backing claims that white law-enforcement officers kidnapped and sexually assaulted Tawana Brawley. Sharpton offered some insider "scoops," maintaining that half a dozen white males were with Tawana over four days in November 1987, transporting her through wooded areas of Wappingers Falls, New York.

Some of what Sharpton said to Nobile seemed to come from Mars. According to the reverend, the attackers were part of a sadistic cult. One reason the teenager did not have serious bruises, Sharpton maintained, was that the cult did not beat victims. Rather, they supposedly did things like force Tawana to drink a "milky substance" that was not drugs but that made her dozy. In the *Spin* article, Sharpton is quoted as saying, "The fact that they let her eat and bathe doesn't mean that she was well treated. She was not on a vacation at the Hilton Hotel in Nassau, the Bahamas. We're talking about cultism."

Sharpton went on to say he and Black attorneys Alton Maddox and C. Vernon Mason had names of area residents who knew of that alleged cult and who were willing to talk. Such residents never surfaced. One complicating factor in the Brawley case was that one of the accused men, Harry Crist, a part-time police officer, committed suicide. It was after the suicide was reported in the local press that the Brawley team began claiming that Crist had been among the attackers. Those who knew him personally maintained that Crist had killed himself because he was depressed.

Nobile's article was published two months before Payne's *Newsday* article. Therefore, Nobile did not have the firm evidence presented by Payne that the Brawley accusations were a fraud. But the *Spin* article was extremely significant in the unraveling of the Brawley case in later years. It played a major role in the successful 1998 defamation suit filed by Steven Pagones, a former Dutchess County prosecutor, against Sharpton, Maddox, and Mason. The trio had maintained that Pagones was among white law-enforcement types who had sexually assaulted Tawana. Pagones's suit relied in good part on a 367-page transcription of Nobile's 1987 *Spin* interview with Sharpton.

Nobile gained wide attention in the early 2000s for his campaign against popular radio host Don Imus for Imus's tendency to disparage

Blacks, such as when he referred to Rutgers University's women's basketball players as "nappy-headed hos" (i.e., whores). *Spin*, the magazine, ceased publication in 2012, though there is still a spin.com music news website.

Rev. Al Moved on, Leaving Former Partners Behind

Sharpton has effectively put his Brawley past behind him. The experience, in fact, may have even helped him, as he continued to bolster his seemingly natural talents for drawing the attention of the mainstream media. Indeed, many in the Black community continued to connect viscerally with the arguments on behalf of Brawley. This is attributable to a shared gut anger at centuries of rapes and other abuses of Black women in America.

The Tawana Brawley storm left Rev. Sharpton as a survivor, but it effectively destroyed the career paths of his two Brawley partners, attorneys C. Vernon Mason and Alton Maddox.

Mason had once seemed destined for a significant and maybe even powerful future on the New York political scene. In 1985 he impressed observers and political pundits when he made a creditable showing as he attempted to unseat one of the longest-serving prosecutors in New York City history. That prosecutor was Robert Morgenthau, scion of a renowned political family.

In an editorial on September 2, 1985, the *New York Times* wrote that "[a]fter 10 years as District Attorney for Manhattan, Robert Morgenthau faces his first serious opponent" in C. Vernon Mason. The *Times* went on to say that "the challenge inspires healthy discussion of this powerful office and the way Mr. Morgenthau has filled it." The paper argued that Morgenthau had "fumbled the grand-jury proceedings" against Bernhard Goetz, the white techie who fired an unlicensed pistol at four Black youngsters on a subway, gravely wounding one, because he "thought" they were going to rob him. But in the very last paragraphs of its editorial, the *Times* said that despite significant criticisms of the prosecutor, the paper was endorsing Morgenthau.

Mason, a graduate of Columbia University Law School, was highly regarded in the Black New York City community. Blacks came out in large numbers to vote for Mason on September 10, 1985, in the Democratic primary for Manhattan prosecutor. Mason lost, but he garnered a third of the vote—which was considered a major achievement and a sign that great achievements were waiting in Mason's future. There had never been—and as of mid-2021 has not been—a Black person elected as prosecutor in Manhattan.

But three years after that election, in the thick of the Brawley case, Mason fell under the light of constant, piercing attention from the press and the New York court system. It was eventually determined that he had overcharged and mistreated poor clients, and a panel of the New York State Appellate Division in 1995 disbarred him.

Mason went on to become a deacon at Harlem's esteemed Abyssinian Baptist Church and a teacher and administrator at New York Theological Seminary.

As for Alton Maddox, his license to practice law was suspended. That was because he would not appear at a State Bar disciplinary hearing to explain his conduct in the Brawley case. He had refused during the Brawley episode to cooperate with appointed prosecutors who were trying to uncover what had happened. He never cooperated with those state officials, and his license to practice law in New York has remained suspended.

Maddox has suffered far more than Mason. Attempts to reach him in Georgia, which is his last known residence I'm aware of, were not successful. "I make every effort to avoid listening to Rev. Al Sharpton on radio or television," Maddox wrote in a 2015 posting on his website, universityofaltonmaddox.com. Another time that year, Maddox wrote dismissively that Sharpton might "someday succeed former

Mayor David N. Dinkins as 'Head Negro in Charge' in New York and amass a fortune."

As for money owed to Pagones after his defamation suit against them: Sharpton was told to give Pagones $65,000, which some of his financially comfortable Black supporters paid on his behalf; and Maddox and Mason began turning over what they owed (respectively $95,000 and $185,000) in segments into the twenty-first century. Maddox has from time to time publicly repeated his old claims that Pagones was involved in an attack on Tawana Brawley. Mason has been silent.

Sharpton has not backed off the original rape allegations—but he hedges. Sharpton told me in 2020 that everything he said about Tawana Brawley in the late 1980s came his way via Alton Maddox. He said that, at that time, he trusted what Maddox was saying about the case, because Maddox was the Brawley family's attorney.

"He [Maddox] was the one that told us [about Pagones]," Sharpton said, speaking by phone as he was being driven from a church in New Jersey, heading back to New York to do his Sunday MSNBC *PoliticsNation* program. Sharpton added that Maddox in recent decades "went all the way extreme" in his public statements about Brawley and other matters.

Sharpton said he still believed there was reason back then to make a legal case that Tawana Brawley had been attacked. "I believe that there was enough of a *prima facia* case for it all to come out in court," he said.

I also asked Sharpton about Maddox's website postings saying that the Reverend wants to be New York City's "Head Negro in Charge." Sharpton said civil rights remains his calling and that Maddox in the 1990s kept denouncing many Black leaders and they simply began avoiding him.

3

⣿

The Early '80s:
Sharpton Enters the Realm
Where White Newspapers Ruled

THE STORY OF Rev. Al's relationship with the white press begins in 1984. He was not yet the boisterous presence he would become, but he was stepping onto the stage. In the spring of 2020 Sharpton told attendees at the Saturday meeting of his National Action Network that they should watch a "Trial by Media" documentary. He said he was surprised that there was video of him protesting in those days. The documentary, one of a number in a "Trial by Media" series, was titled *Subway Vigilante*. It showed Sharpton leading angry and noisy protesters, denouncing the Manhattan prosecutor's handling of the Bernhard Goetz case. Many Blacks felt that Goetz was not prosecuted with the vigor the case deserved. Goetz, in December 1984, shot four Black young men he believed were trying to rob him on the subway. Most New York City journalists knew little to nothing of Al Sharpton at that moment.

In 1983, a year before the Bernhard Goetz story, there was a precursor white-on-Black killing, but Sharpton wasn't among the notable fist-raisers. Other Blacks were noisier and more visible.

On September 15, 1983, Michael Stewart, a twenty-five-year-old Black artist from Brooklyn, was stopped and arrested by city transit police officers for scrawling graffiti at the subway station at 14th

Street and First Avenue in Manhattan. Police officers said that Stewart fought them. Bruised, battered, and hogtied, Stewart was taken by police to Bellevue Hospital, where he died several days later.

The Black weekly *Amsterdam News* stood out for the attention it gave the Stewart case. Its reporter Peter Noel wrote one passionate article after another on it. Noel wrote in a flowing narrative style, and his stories also revealed the outrage of a people. He conveyed the anguish and frustration of Blacks in New York, culminating in the acquittals of the police officers by an all-white jury.

A search of the Proquest database turned up forty-four articles by Noel mentioning Michael Stewart, between Stewart's death in 1983 and the November 1985 acquittals of all six policers officers involved. Brooklyn Pentecostal minister Rev. Herbert Daughtry displayed disgust in comments he made to Noel. "It appeared some elements in the Transit Police Department are vying with others in the New York City Police Department to see who are the most brutal cops," Daughtry was quoted by Noel as saying, in a September 13, 1986, *Amsterdam* article. "Why shouldn't we react with fury . . . ?" Daughtry asked. (Note: The city's Transit Police merged with the New York City Police Department in 1995.)

In November 1985, a jury acquitted the six transit officers who had been charged. Louis Clayton Jones, one of the Black attorneys representing the Stewart family, told reporters outside the Manhattan Supreme Court building: "And all the players happened to be white. The six defendants, the six defense lawyers, the two prosecutors, the 12 jurors, the judge, and even every court officer in the well of the courtroom was white. The only black person there was the victim, and he was unable to testify, unfortunately." (That quote was in a November 25, 1985, *New York Times* article by Isabel Wilkerson.)

The white press perhaps did show progress in its sensitivities to racial injustices, as it gave some attention to the Michael Stewart killing in 1983. But it was nothing like the coverage they would give to Black-on-white violence, real and questionable, three years later. That was when Al Sharpton began making an art form of attracting the attention of journalists with white newspapers.

Craft Was King

Sharpton (like most people) would not have been aware of it, but he was entering the arena as the daily print media were peaking in their dominance in New York and other big cities around the country. The press commanded respect, in terms of political might, economic significance, and influence with the populace. That populace was still mostly white, largely of immigrant Italian, Jewish, or Irish descent. And in the 1970s and '80s, owning or working for a New York City newspaper was like having a badge of power and respectability in your pocket.

Dollar values of newspapers had soared to a point where ownership was no longer just a matter of ideology or influence with local politicians. Newspapers had become go-to places for corporate financial advisers and greedy entrepreneurs. In 1967 the *New York Times* went public, which is to say that its shares were traded on Wall Street (even though the Sulzberger family retained percentage control).

As this happened throughout the industry, an animal-like determination to get rid of competitors became stronger. And a key to the doors of the cash was advertising. As Rev. Al began courting their attention, New York City's newspapers were proud displays of the profession of journalism—or as many, if not all, reporters preferred to call it, the craft of journalism.

Reporters and photographers at *New York Newsday* and other city papers were members of a union, the Newspaper Guild, later renamed the NewsGuild. But despite their identification with everyday working men and women, journalists of that era lived fairly comfortable lives. They were beneficiaries of a certain largesse of many newspaper owners.

In my first months at *New York Newsday*, it seemed money all but floated in the air of the newsroom, including reimbursements for drinks and dinners with sources and even lunch with colleagues.

When I was working on *Newsday*'s national and foreign desks on Long Island, I received a phone call, a "tip," about a newsworthy happening expected in Haiti. I decided I should fly there that night. I needed some cash. So I walked into the office of Tony Marro, the top editor. Tony listened to my sixty-second spiel and reached into his wallet, pulling out five $100 bills. "Be safe," he said as he handed me the money. I thanked him and left.

At another time, I had to travel to Haiti during a U.S.-imposed trade embargo, when no American credit cards could be used. *Newsday* gave me $15,000 in cash. I carried the money in a thin pouch concealed under my *guayabera* (Cuban shirt), and I drove and walked through villages around the poverty-stricken country, making discreet payments to anyone who helped me with my reporting needs.

Back in New York City, reporters knew that the stories which boosted circulation—and ad dollars—were ones that made "the wood." The "wood" was old craft talk for the front page of the tabloid papers. By the late 1980s, the guy who could be counted on for quotes and stories making the wood was Al Sharpton.

Tell It to Sweeney

At the *New York Daily News*, there was a saying among the reporters: "Tell it to Sweeney." It was advice for young reporters trying to climb the ladder of recognition and get a decent number of bylines and nice "play," which meant having your stories on pages five, three, or maybe even "the wood." Sweeney was the surname meant to represent the average working-class New Yorker. And in the early and midcentury decades, that average "Joe" and his wife, "Mary," were readers of Irish heritage. "Telling it to Sweeney" meant being straightforward in the crafting of your sentences, being relevant to the lives of your readers, being funny when you could. Being empathetic with Sweeney.

Most of all, to successfully perform their craft, reporters had to find sources who gave them words that flowed, maybe even alliterative ones, crafted in the writing with clear references to the overarching stories or sub-stories. As every good politician knew, anger, when vented with the authenticity of a practiced actor, could win over scribes who were standing at press conferences, pens or pencils in one hand moving speedily as they scribbled what they were hearing onto oblong reporters' notebooks resting in the other hand. (Of course, when a story drew really manic attention, TV reporters would be at the press conferences, too. And for them, well-done, attention-grabbing remarks from the source came to be known as "sound bites.")

Most of the reporters who went full blast after Rev. Al in his rise to fame (or, as some would have said, infamy) were old-school white fellows. They were craft descendants of the style that shaped tabloid journalism just before and after World War II. New York City and its borough of Brooklyn were mostly Irish, Italian, and Jewish. And the Irish in particular held strong sway in the rooms where it happened, where decisions concerning politics and the criminal justice system were made.

Of course, New York City eventually began to shift in decennial Census numbers from overwhelmingly white to heavily Black. By the time Rev. Al was being widely seen and heard, New York City was a Black/white place, with the next rising ethnic group being Latinos, who were mostly Puerto Ricans in those days. (Mexicans and others from Central and South America, as well as Muslims, did not show themselves notably in the neighborhoods and workplaces until the late 1990s.)

The Irish mentality shined in the writing of the most successful tabloid columnists (who made the most money, hundreds of thousands a year, by the last decades of the century). Among them were Jimmy Breslin and Pete Hamill, both now deceased. Breslin, a college dropout, wrote columns about everyday men and women and was an early "progressive" in the treatment he gave to Black New

Yorkers. He liked to think of himself as one who "climbed stairs," rather than just making phone calls and reading background "clips" of old stories pulled from the files by newsroom librarians. He'd go to the apartment of the person whose thoughts and words he needed.

In the thick of the times when Sharpton was just becoming known to reporters and readers, Breslin literally climbed the stairs of a public housing building in the Bronx and got details about the October 29, 1984, police killing of a mentally disabled and elderly Black woman. Her name was Eleanor Bumpurs. New York City cops had gone to Bumpurs's apartment after having received phone calls that she was showing signs of emotional distress. It was Breslin's interview with a neighbor—who had heard the encounter between Bumpurs and the cops—that led to big headlines and, ultimately, the charging of police officer Stephen Sullivan with second-degree manslaughter. He had fired two shells from a 12-gauge shotgun at Bumpurs, one of them hitting her in the chest and killing her.

Of course, Sullivan was ultimately acquitted. That's the way things were—and, sadly, are.

It must be noted, in reflecting on Breslin, how dramatically his behavior on one occasion revealed the sexism and racism that were still sometimes on the surface in those days. In 1990, Breslin walked into the *New York Newsday* newsroom in Manhattan spewing anger at a young female Korean-American reporter who had complained to an editor that one of Breslin's recent columns was sexist. Breslin, loudly and angrily, called the reporter, Ji-Yeon Yuh, a "slant-eyed . . . bitch." Yuh was not in the newsroom at the time. Breslin apologized and was suspended for two weeks, but he returned to writing his column and books, retiring in 2004. (He had stayed on at *Long Island Newsday* after *New York Newsday* closed in 1995.)

As for Hamill, he wrote books that stood out for their literary beauty, and he also conveyed an image of himself as one who identified with those on the streets, those who were left out of the rooms where the power brokers met. He was different from Breslin in that Hamill was also something of a Hollywood-type personality. He dated Jacqueline Kennedy (later Onassis), widow of the biggest Irish politician of them all, the assassinated President John F. Kennedy. In the context of this book, it would be wrong to leave out that Hamill ran notably with the crowd of white reporters and city residents in their fuming reactions attacking the five Black and Latino boys who were accused in the 1989 sex attack on a white "Central Park jogger" and were later found through DNA and other evidence to have not been involved in the attack. In 2011, the nonprofit journalism group the Poynter Institute published a reflection on the Central Park case written by Julia Dahl, who pointed out that Hamill had written that the arrested boys came "from a world of crack, welfare, guns, knives, indifference and ignorance . . . a land with no fathers . . . to smash, hurt, rob, stomp, rape. The enemies were rich. The enemies were white."

(More reflections on the Central Park Five come in Chapter 4, "Black Women and the Embedded Racism of the Realm.")

Mike McAlary

For me, it was Mike McAlary who exemplified the collective personality of the white tabloid media as it put Al Sharpton front and center on the stage. Brash but friendly, he hung out in bars where reporters went to share beer and tales about the funny things that had happened on their way to their latest stories. McAlary showed old-school Irish New York in his speaking style, his ease in chatting with friends, news sources, and anyone he happened to run into on the street. This style showed itself even though he had been born in Honolulu, where his father served in the Navy. He spent part of his childhood in Brooklyn (Flatbush) and then moved with his family to New Hampshire before going to Syracuse University in upstate New York to study journalism. He put himself on a path to star status when he took a job as a reporter at *New York Newsday* in the mid-1980s.

One of the biggest advantages Irish reporters had in those days was that they could acquire personal ties to brass in the New York City Police Department, who were heavily Irish. McAlary's strongest suit in the late 1980s was his coverage of cops, including a scandal that ruined (any remaining) perceptions of everyday precinct-working officers as honest and dedicated to the good of the communities they served. His exposé was a mini-revival of the famed Frank Serpico story of the early 1970s.

Using his sources, McAlary revealed patterns of extortion by police officers concentrated largely at the 77th police precinct, which took in the heavily Black Brooklyn neighborhoods of Crown Heights and Bedford-Stuyvesant. Cops there were ripping off drug pushers by demanding some of the money from the deals they made. After doing a series of articles, McAlary wrote a book titled *Buddy Boys*, and he began establishing himself as one of the best "stair-climbing" and politically connected scribes in the business.

⣿

Here's where Rev. Al comes in. In January 1988, when I was off in Haiti for *Newsday* covering the political unrest there, McAlary and his investigative team did a story that shook the city, especially its Black communities. It was all about undercover dealings of the Rev. Al Sharpton and the FBI. It had a major impact on Sharpton's life.

The piece laid bare that federal investigators had pulled Rev. Al into their circle in 1983. In secret meetings, top FBI investigators used sketchy information to scare Sharpton into thinking they could bring drug charges against him if he didn't cooperate with them. The charges were not that he used or sold drugs but that he had some kind of connection to the trade. The Feds said they wanted him to go after some of the people he had links to and to record evidence that could be used in criminal cases. Among those they wanted was the big-time boxing promoter Don King. Sharpton had gotten to know King through James Brown, the "Godfather of Soul," with whom Sharpton had traveled the country and the world, helping promote Brown's performances. Brown and Sharpton had a long-lasting father–son relationship that is fundamental to an understanding of Sharpton's character development. (It is explored later in the book.)

In those days, the early 1980s, when they reached out to Rev. Al, the Feds were snooping around the country, especially New York, trying to entrap actual or suspected Black revolutionaries. From further press reports and my conversation with one of the FBI agents, it seems clear that Sharpton nodded in the affirmative that he would help with that. Photos of one of those 1983 meetings, leaked to journalists in the early 2000s, showed a fear in Sharpton's face that contrasted sharply with the young preacher's public personality.

The *Newsday* scoop bore the headline "The Minister and the Feds." It began on page 1, the wood. An accompanying article, starting on page 5, was "Sharpton's Mob Dealings." That story led to an understanding that Sharpton had developed—largely through his work with performing artists—relationships with organized-crime figures who played roles in the heavily Black music industry. The *Newsday* stories of January 20, 1988, were tasty mind-food for newspaper readers in New York City, as well as those around the country. And with TV and radio expanding the reach, it was the talk of evening newscasts.

There were strong suspicions in New York City, among Black politicians and others, that Rev. Al was toast, that his credibility had been mortally wounded. What perhaps was especially hurtful to Rev. Al was the disclosure in *Newsday* that Sharpton had been using a telephone provided by federal investigators to record conversations. The newspaper also told readers he had made reports of electoral wrongdoing, allegedly committed by widely respected Black Brooklyn politicians (who had also had political run-ins with Rev. Al in the past).

One of those politicians was Al Vann, then a member of the New York Assembly, who had come up as a radical leader of the African American Teachers Association in the 1960s. Vann then embarked on a career of progressive politics that finally resulted in his winning election to the Assembly. (He held different elective offices representing his Bedford-Stuyvesant community from the mid-1970s through 2013, when he retired from the New York City Council.) Vann came up during an era when other local Black politicians were being convicted of crimes related to their conduct in office. Vann would often note with pride that he had never been convicted of, or even charged with, a crime—other than participating in street protests.

The other politician said to have been an object of Sharpton's exchanges with Feds was Major Owens. Owens had been a congressman representing Central Brooklyn since 1982 and was a darling of Black and white anti-machine progressives.

The *Newsday* article was published the day after the paper's reporters had interviewed Sharpton at his Brooklyn office. According to the article, "Sharpton told *Newsday* that he has cooperated in investigations of election-related irregularities involving Rep. Major Owens (D-Brooklyn) and Assemblyman Al Vann (D-Brooklyn), as well as investigations involving organized crime."

Some Blacks lost faith in Rev. Al. Later that year, in June, I got a call from several Black activists who said they'd always had suspicions about the preacher and unloaded to me about their relationships with him in the early 1980s. The activists had been impressed with my own scoop of a year before, for which I had spent a week interviewing fugitive Black revolutionary Assata Shakur in Cuba. I met with those activists and wrote the story that was published in *Newsday* as "The Minister and the Fugitive."

One of those who knew and identified with Shakur was Ahmed Obafemi, whom I quoted in Chapter 1, where he said he did not believe Sharpton was a changed man in 2020 but rather was a "con man" just as he had been in the 1980s.

In April 2014, while I was teaching journalism at Brooklyn College, I interviewed Obafemi for a Sharpton article I was writing for the *Daily News*. Obafemi told me he had vivid memories of Sharpton back in 1983—the year Sharpton was known to have been under pressure from the FBI to locate Black revolutionaries. Obafemi said Sharpton was always carrying a briefcase and that he strongly suspected Sharpton was recording conversations with wires tucked inside the briefcase. My article was published on April 13 with the headline "Al Sharpton and His Bugged Briefcase." A former *Village Voice* reporter, William Bastone, had reported on April 8, 2014, that Sharpton had in fact been using a wired briefcase as a confidential informant for the Feds. Bastone had obtained government affadavits backing up his reporting, which was published on his Smoking Gun website.

Obafemi and others remain to this day disgusted by Sharpton's behavior in the 1980s.

Progressive Black elected officials also became leery of Sharpton, in 1988, when *Newsday* broke its story about Sharpton's recording conversations on his bugged phone line. Among the politicians who felt stung was Roger Green. Green was then New York state assemblyman.

In a phone conversation with me in 2020, Green recalled hearing about Sharpton's bugged phone and becoming nervous. As the story came out, Green was participating with Sharpton and others in a "Days of Outrage" protest. "I had been in the same jail cell with Sharpton," Green said. "When [that Sharpton] story broke I remember the feeling of a kind of betrayal."

Green said he was not soothed when Sharpton, reacting to the *Newsday* story, went "on TV and said his phone was bugged but that he was only using [the bugged phone line] for drug dealers [who could then be busted by law-enforcement officials]."

Green added: "So if the FBI hears my voice or Rev. [Herbert] Daughtry's voice, are they going to say, 'Hey, let's shut this off'?" Green said his unease was felt "particularly by those of us who had experiences with COINTELPRO." COINTELPRO, or the Counterintelligence Program, had been set up by the FBI to monitor the activities and conversations of Black radicals around the country. The program had been kept secret for decades, but by the 1980s its existence was public knowledge.

(The Rev. Herbert Daughtry, to whom Green referred, had been, through the 1970s and '80s, one of the most outspoken activists against police violence against Blacks in Brooklyn. Daughtry was then, and remains, pastor of the House of the Lord Pentecostal Church located near Downtown Brooklyn.)

Green expounded on his thoughts about Sharpton. "I'm one who believes a person is capable of maturity. . . . They can change the way they live. As Amiri Baraka [the late Black nationalist and renowned poet], said, 'Under every wig there can be a growing consciousness.'"

Baraka's "wig" reference was a simile for the processed James Brown–like hairdo that Sharpton sported at the time. Black militants of the 1970s and '80s frowned upon straightened, "conked" hair styles, saying they were dismissive of the natural beauty of people of African descent.

"Our leaders are human and capable of human foibles. I think Sharpton has definitely matured," said Green, who in 2020 was doing research and activism on Black community-health needs. These days, Sharpton's hair, as seen on MSNBC and all over the country, is still a bit slicked back, but not James Brown long and flamboyant, as it once was.

⁞⁞⁞

New York Newsday was acknowledged, properly, as the newspaper that published the first story about Rev. Al's dealings with the FBI and mob figures. That package of *Newsday* articles appeared in the paper on January 20, 1988. But two weeks later, on February 2, 1988, *The Village Voice*, an alternative weekly newspaper, came out with its own deeply reported examinations of Sharpton and his past links with the federal government. Those two articles, totaling roughly 5,000 words, contained details similar to ones in *Newsday*, but they stood out notably for subjective insertions of phrases and sentences regarding Sharpton's perceived character. The main story, for instance, ended with a description of Sharpton as a "flimflam imposter and provocateur." That article was headlined "The Hustler."

A much shorter article was based on an interview with a man reported as having been at two of the meetings attended by Sharpton, federal agents, and undercover informants. The *Voice* thus displayed its cachet in investigative reporting. Two of the bylines were of reporters who would go on to do significant writing about Sharpton and his associates, those two being Jack Newfield and William (Bill) Bastone. Bastone became known as one of the city's most informed journalists regarding organized-crime figures. Interestingly, the *Voice* bylines on the February 2 pieces did not include that of *Voice* reporter Wayne Barrett, who over the decades would stand out for continual questioning of Sharpton's motives and character.

Showing Ability to Bond with Reporters Who Had Slammed Him

Rev. Al Sharpton began to show his strongest signs of change in January 1991. That was immediately after an incident that made him believe he might die, then and there, at the age of thirty-six.

For months, Sharpton had been leading huge demonstrations in the largely Italian neighborhood of Bensonhurst in Brooklyn. The boisterous marches were set off by the murder of a Black teenager, Yusuf Hawkins. Hawkins had been in the neighborhood with a few friends hoping to see a used car they had learned about through an ad. A white mob attacked the young men, killing Yusuf Hawkins.

After that incident, Sharpton put together busloads of protesters who traveled from Central Brooklyn and elsewhere into Bensonhurst. The protests continued for months.

As one of the protests, on January 12, 1991, was beginning, an angry Bensonhurst resident, Michael Riccardi, plunged a five-inch knife into Sharpton's chest. The demonstration halted in the confusion. Sharpton was driven to Coney Island Hospital.

It had been known that Sharpton might be targeted for violence. Angry white residents of Bensonhurst had been shouting vile racial insults, like "Niggers, go home!"; tossing pieces of watermelon at the protesters; and making threats over the five months of the protests. (There had been similar reactions in the Howard Beach section of Queens, where Sharpton had led demonstrations following the December 1986 killing of Michael Griffith. Griffith, who was twenty-three years old and Black, had been walking through Howard Beach with two friends when a gang of whites set upon them. The whites chased Griffith onto a parkway, where he was hit by a car and killed.)

Sharpton, as we all know, survived the 1991 knife attack. To some Sharpton supporters, the attack was a validation of assertions that he was a successor to Rev. Martin Luther King Jr. and Malcolm X, the Black leaders assassinated in the 1960s.

Sharpton, indeed, displayed evidence of a coming transformation. In March 1992, he showed up at the sentencing of twenty-eight-year-old Michael Riccardi, the man who had stabbed him in Bensonhurst, and told Judge Francis X. Egitto that Riccardi was "the kind of guy who needs programs where he can be reformed. . . . There is a need to be healed." Afterward, outside the courtroom, Sharpton told reporters, "I did only what Dr. King would have done."

Sharpton's comments were reported in a March 16, 1992, *New York Newsday* article written by Patricia Hurtado. Riccardi received a sentence of from five to fifteen years and was released from prison in January 2001. Sharpton in 2003 received $200,000 from New York City, after having filed a lawsuit saying the city had been delinquent in not giving him adequate protection during the Bensonhurst demonstrations, according to stories in the *Times*, the *New York Post*, and other papers published on December 9, 2003. Representing Sharpton in his civil suit against the city was Sanford Rubenstein, who would be at Sharpton's side many times during the early years of the twenty-first century, standing with Black victims of police brutality. Some critics of Sharpton would denounce the relationship with Rubenstein, whom they called a money-hungry ambulance chaser. Sharpton always denied that Rubenstein gave money to Sharpton or to the National Action Network, which Sharpton had started in the months following the Bensonhurst stabbing.

Back when Sharpton was in the hospital recovering from the proce-
dures performed after the stabbing, he was visited by family members, close friends, and others. With one of the visitors, Sharpton
showed an ease that augured well for a future of meaningful and
mutually beneficial relationships.

That visitor was Mike McAlary, the Irish-descended tabloid guy
who put the match to Sharpton's reputation in January 1988, with the
news-breaking story about "the Minister and the Feds."

"I always wanted you to shut up, but not like this," McAlary told
Sharpton, according to Sharpton's recollection of the visit.

McAlary was far from the only one to show humor while Sharpton
was in the hospital. Shocked by the news of what had happened, Rev.
Jesse Jackson—the civil rights activist, former presidential candidate,
and father-figure of Sharpton's—was one of the first to call the hospital. Jackson told Sharpton that, more than anything else, it was his
very fat torso that saved his life that day in Bensonhurst, blocking the
knife from ripping through the heart's arteries.

But it was that exchange with Mike McAlary which perhaps most
revealed changes taking place inside Sharpton.

The developing tenderness between the protester and the reporter
did not end in 1991. Two years later, McAlary was driving along the
FDR (the Franklin Delano Roosevelt) Drive, on the east side of
Manhattan. His Volvo sedan skidded and then slammed into a bar-
rier dividing the highway from the service road. McAlary suffered
serious injuries to his head, chest, and abdomen and was taken to
Bellevue Hospital in critical condition.

McAlary survived, and while he was in recovery, Sharpton went
to visit him.

"I always wanted you to stop writing, but not like this," the Rev.
told McAlary. Sharpton recalled that 1993 visit five years later, when
he spoke at a 1998 memorial service for McAlary, who had passed
away of colon cancer, just after his forty-second birthday.

Earlier that year, months before his death, McAlary won a Pulitzer Prize. It was for one of the greatest scoops of the 1990s. It revealed that a city police officer, Justin Volpe, had shoved a nightstick up the rectum of a Haitian man named Abner Louima and did so right at the 70th precinct police station in Brooklyn. McAlary was receiving chemotherapy in August 1997 when, after getting a tip from a source, he went to Brooklyn's Coney Island Hospital to interview Louima. "They said, 'Take this, nigger,' and stuck the stick in my rear end," Louima told the dying but note-taking McAlary, whose city-rocking scoop of a story was published in the *Daily News* the next day, August 13, 1997, with the headline "The Frightful Whisperings from a Coney Island Bed."

Volpe was convicted of violating Louima's civil rights and was sentenced to thirty years in federal prison. (Volpe is slated for release in 2025.)

In an interview with me in the summer of 2020, Sharpton said McAlary stood out for him in a positive way among reporters who covered the Reverend for white news outlets. "The one I give credit to is Mike McAlary. Mike McAlary said the story [of Sharpton's working with the FBI] didn't make sense, because you had to know you didn't agree to nothin'. Sittin' up there hearing a proposition is not agreein' to somethin' . . . ." The comments, made to me during a phone chat in 2020, showed Sharpton's ability to put a spin on the past, using words and tonality to make a statement that the words alone don't seem to say.

Sharpton must have been aware of a truth very evident to me: that the best of reporters, especially the white ones covering Blacks, could be as calculating as Rev. Al. They intently managed their relationships with sources, getting them to feel comfortable so that they might give them great quotes and maybe some tidbits that could lead to front-page scoops.

McAlary is long gone, but in 2014 one of his old *Newsday* colleagues wrote a little reflection on him. It referred to the story McClary and his team did on Sharpton and the FBI, decades back.

That old colleague of McAlary's was Richard Esposito. Like so many of the old-time newspaper reporters, Esposito had gone on to other jobs in the twenty-first century. In 2014 he was working for NBC as senior executive producer of the network's News Investigative Unit. He saw a bit of irony in the fact that Rev. Al was hosting a news show at the related company MSNBC.

"We pass each other in the halls, and I've appeared on his broadcast, where he introduced me as 'my colleague, Richard Esposito,'" Esposito wrote, with a tone of humous irony, in an NBC web article titled "Rev. Al Sharpton and Me."

Referring to the 1988 *Newsday* scoop that told of Rev. Al's meetings with the Feds and his bugged phone line, Esposito wrote: "McAlary . . . was jumping for joy after he and [fellow lead-reporter Bob] Drury completed the interview with Sharpton. . . . McAlary felt he'd nailed 'The Rev.'"

Yes, looking back, we can say that many reporters in the late 1980s felt they'd "nailed" Rev. Al. After all, he had gone boldly against the advice repeated by politicians and journalists through the twentieth century: Never get into a fight with someone who buys ink by the barrel. That legendary warning reflected the often-feared power of old American newspapers. It was attributed to Mark Twain, but whatever the source, it became passed-down American wisdom. Sharpton once flouted that advice with pursed lips. Then he seemed to have found wisdom in it.

In 2020, Richard Esposito was named Deputy Commissioner for Public Information for the New York City Police Department.

Black Journalist, Hurt Professionally While Sharpton Survived

Earl Caldwell had reason to view newspapers as rank with race-based double standards. Caldwell was born in rural Pennsylvania in the mid-1930s, though he told me he's not 100 percent sure of the year because it varies in archival records. As a cub reporter in the 1960s, Caldwell worked for the now-defunct *New York Herald Tribune* and then for the *New York Post* (which was fairly liberal in those days) before getting hired by the *New York Times*. As a reporter with the *Times* in 1968, he was the only journalist with the Rev. Martin Luther King Jr. at the Lorraine Motel when a bullet fired from a rooming house across the street hit King and ended the life of the leader of the civil rights movement. Caldwell became known the world over and had to fend off requests from other reporters to be their source for stories.

It might be argued that in the history of the American press Caldwell has a chapter that stands alone. Besides the King assassination, he gained attention for his stories on the Black Panther Party in the late '60s, while he was based in California with the *Times*.

In doing his Panther stories, it became evident to Caldwell that the FBI was not only going after the gun-carrying, black beret–wearing Panthers, but after Earl Caldwell himself. The Feds wanted him to turn over information he was receiving from his Panther Party sources, including names and contact information. Some of the sources, of course, had spoken to him "on background," meaning he had committed himself to not revealing who they were. Caldwell was clear with the Feds. No way would he turn over to them information about his sources.

In 1970 the U.S. Circuit Court of Appeals in San Francisco ruled in Caldwell's favor, although the U.S Supreme Court afterward rejected his arguments. In the end, the Caldwell case led to significant victories for reporters and First Amendment advocates. Determined to defend the freedom of the press, state legislatures around the nation began to pass "shield laws." Those acts protected reporters from having to reveal sources attained as they carried out their journalist duties.

In 1974 Caldwell left the *New York Times*, and in 1979 he became the first Black to write a regular column at a white New York City newspaper. That was the *New York Daily News*. And one of the biggest stories he would write about was the Tawana Brawley episode.

In an interview in the summer of 2020, Caldwell told me he identified with Tawana Brawley's upstate New York family, because he'd been raised in a similarly rural section of Pennsylvania where whites believed they could do anything to Black girls and get away with it. His *Daily News* columns showed strong empathies with the Brawleys and Tawana's three advisers, Mason, Maddox, and Sharpton.

But by 1989, Caldwell began to feel angst about the growing consensus, even in the Black community, that Tawana Brawley's rape allegations were not just wrong, but also manufactured. He began to experience an inner pain, a feeling of having been let down by activists he'd trusted and given so much support to in his columns.

"I didn't realize the extent to which I was being used," he told me, referring especially to Brawley adviser C. Vernon Mason, with whom he had worked closely in previous years.

"The Tawana Brawley thing changed everything. . . . That case really ended my time at the *Daily News*," Caldwell said.

In addition to that, Caldwell was experiencing the stresses of working at a paper—the *News*—at which some longtime Black journalists had filed a joint discrimination suit. Those Black reporters and editors won their case in a federal court in Manhattan in 1987, just several months before Tawana Brawley said she was raped. Some of the Blacks at the *Daily News* suffered deep psychological pain as a result of the case, resulting from personalized battles with editors at the *News*. (As I write this, only one of the four Black plaintiffs is alive, and he, Causewell Vaughan, has led a life of remarkable recovery from those challenges. A native of the Caribbean island of

Jamaica, he did public relations work for a time with Jamaica-born Brooklyn politician Una Clarke, and he then went on to serve with distinction as editor-in-chief of the *Daily Challenge*, a Black newspaper based in Brooklyn.)

The Rockaway Five

In the mid-1990s, Sharpton and another activist minister, Rev. Timothy Mitchell, were leading protests outside the offices of Queens District Attorney Richard A. Brown, demanding that Brown prosecute a New York City police officer accused of sexually assaulting several Black livery cab drivers. The episode was called the Rockaway Five case, referring to that heavily Black section of Queens.

When Caldwell wrote a column about the Rockaway Five in 1994, he says, a white editor complained about the article. The editor refused to run it unless Caldwell made changes. Caldwell refused to make the changes the editor wanted. He left the paper, never to return. He told me he's not sure whether it should be said that he was fired or just resigned. But his long newspaper reporting career was over.

⋮⋮

Sharpton suffered no ill effects from the Rockaway Five case. But Caldwell sank to low points of his life. He had little money and was about to be evicted from his Manhattan apartment. He told me that Eutrice Leid, former managing editor of the *City Sun* weekly newspaper, a pro-Sharpton Black newspaper based in Brooklyn, put out the word—to Black politicians and others—that Caldwell needed help.

Caldwell told me that, soon after Leid began reaching out, Al Sharpton called him.

"He said I want to talk to you about something," Caldwell recalled, referring to Sharpton. "He [Sharpton] said, 'Meet me at 9 o'clock tomorrow morning, at 57th Street and 7th Avenue' or something like that . . . in midtown.

"So I go there the next morning, at the corner he told me to be on. And the next thing I know, a car [chauffeuring Sharpton] pulls up. Sharpton gets out and says, 'Come with me.' And we go into a bank. He says, 'I got to do a piece of business. You wait right here.' Then he comes back and says, 'I understand you're having a tough time. I want you to take the envelope.' Then he said, 'I've got to go. I've got an appointment.' And he's gone."

Caldwell opened the envelope and found there was $2,500 in cash in it. Was Sharpton paying him for the positive articles in the *Daily News*? Was he displaying his new role of kingmaker in the Black community?

Caldwell had no idea. He didn't call Rev. Al to thank him. He wasn't sure he wanted to thank him. To this day, Caldwell said, he's never reached out to Rev. Al.

He said he is astounded by the life path that Sharpton was able to put himself on.

"It's unfucking real," Caldwell said. "The cat's got nine lives. Sharpton is the one person who walked away from that ordeal [the Tawana Brawley episode] with no more questions being asked."

Mike McAlary and Race-Based Double Standards

Caldwell was especially stung by an irony regarding his departure from the tabloid. It was an irony that, some argued, showed ongoing racial double standards at the *Daily News*. And Sharpton was part of it.

At the same time Caldwell was pushed out at the *Daily News*—because white editors didn't like his column about alleged sex assaults on Black livery van drivers—Mike McAlary was being criticized for a column he had written about a Black woman claiming she had been sexually assaulted in Prospect Park in Brooklyn. McAlary was saying the woman's claims were a fabrication. But whereas Caldwell left the paper for good, McAlary continued writing for the newspaper.

The apparent double standard was noted by William Glaberson of the *New York Times*. Glaberson wrote, ". . . [A]t about the same time [that Caldwell was leaving the *News*], the *News* was publicly defending a white columnist, Mike McAlary, who was widely criticized for writing that a woman who said she had been raped in Prospect Park was perpetrating a hoax." The *Times* article ran on July 18, 1994, as a "Media Business" column. It had the headline: "His Daily News Career Cut Short, Earl Caldwell Sees a Disturbing Racial Divide in Journalism."

Caldwell had committed the journalistic "sin" of not adequately verifying rape charges being made against a police officer. And McAlary had wrongly accused a woman of making up charges that she had been raped. The woman, it was later revealed, was Black and gay. And police eventually acknowledged she had actually been assaulted. In fact, DNA evidence revealed the identity of the attacker. McAlary had written that her allegations of rape had been made up to advance a political agenda. McAlary even compared the victim to Tawana Brawley. The woman became the target of smear campaigns, and she sued McAlary. But a judge determined that while the information was false, McAlary had gotten the information from police sources he believed were reliable and was therefore properly performing his job as a reporter.

Some journalists from the old days suggested McAlary's sources on that rape story were effectively the same sources who fed McAlary information about Al Sharpton's work with the FBI. Except that in the Sharpton matter, the information was accurate.

I reached out to Rev. Sharpton for comment about McAlary's 1994 story wrongly maintaining that the Black woman's rape accusation was a hoax. Sharpton had previously told me of his affection for McAlary, saying he respected him for the truthfulness of his character. Didn't this suggest that Sharpton was excusing behavior many Blacks would say had racist overtones? "McAlary and I never discussed it," Sharpton told me of McAlary's rape hoax column.

In 2018, Fox News's website quoted the Prospect Park rape victim's attorney, Martin Garbus, as saying the victim had suffered greatly from McAlary's mischaracterization of her. "This is a woman who had to live for 23 years with a false accusation of lying, with threats . . . that she was about to be arrested," Garbus said. "It's horrific."

As for Earl Caldwell, he doesn't dwell on his past relationships with Sharpton or New York City's white newspapers. Caldwell is today a writer-in-residence and professor at Hampton University. For a while after leaving the *Daily News*, he worked with the Robert C. Maynard Institute for Journalism Education in Emeryville, California. The Maynard Institute was long dedicated to training journalists of color and trying to increase the number of minorities in the news media. Caldwell also hosted talk-show programs on radio station WBAI. (The Maynard Institute today, lacking substantial funding, is a shadow of its former self.)

4

Black Women and the Embedded Racism of the Realm

BEING A BLACK man who spent two decades working for white newspapers in New York City—first with the *New York Daily News*, then with *Newsday*—there's something I can say with certainty about white newspapers of the Golden Age.

Collectively, they cared little to nothing about rapes of Black women. What took Tawana Brawley to the front pages was the attention-grabbing genius of Rev. Al Sharpton. Nothing more. Nothing.

The contrast between the white press's treatment of assaults on Black women versus attacks on white women was glaring and sickening. At no time was that difference made more manifest than in the case of the Central Park jogger, whose rape defined an era of journalism and of life in New York City.

The victim was Trisha Meili, who was white, from Pennsylvania, and holder of an MBA from Yale. At the time of the April 19, 1989, assault, Meili was working for Salomon Brothers investment bank. She had been grabbed and horribly beaten as she was jogging in Central Park. Police found her in a wooded ravine off a road used by joggers. She was unconscious, her skull fractured, blood from her head mushy in the earth. Taken by ambulance to a hospital, she remained in a coma for almost two weeks. Meili eventually recovered and returned to her job. She had no memory of the brutal attack that almost took her life.

Five Black and Latino teenagers were picked up by police, questioned, and declared suspects. They were charged in the sexual assault and then convicted and sentenced to prison, spending between six and thirteen years behind bars. They became known around the country and the world as the Central Park Five.

Washington Post media critic Howard Kurtz lashed out in print at Sharpton for having shown care for the young men as they were standing trial. Sharpton appeared in the courtroom as an empathetic presence. He made calls for them to receive professional help ensuring their emotional stability. According to Kurtz, the support Sharpton displayed on behalf of those Harlem boys was morally reprehensible. In so declaring, Kurtz cited Sharpton's controversial embracing of Tawana Brawley as she accused white law enforcers in Dutchess County, New York, of raping her. In his *Washington Post* article of September 5, 1990, Kurtz wrote: "Having continued to champion Tawana Brawley's tale of rape and assault long after a grand jury found the claims to be false, Sharpton escorted the teenager [Brawley] to the Central Park jogger trial, where they stood in solidarity with the . . . Harlem youths who were later convicted of brutally raping a white woman."

White reporters, columnists, and editorial writers reacted with rage against the youngsters, and they did so with impulses that almost recalled mindsets of the racialized Reconstruction-era South. In 2011, Julia Dahl, writing for the Poynter Institute, a nonprofit journalism group, cited instances of white city newspapers referring to the Five as "bloodthirsty," "animals," "savages," and "human mutations."

There came also the venomous reaction of the Queens-born realtor and media hound named Donald Trump, who took out newspaper ads saying he wanted the accused five boys executed, before they were even declared guilty. His full-page ad in the *New York Daily News* was published just days after the arrests of the boys. It said:

"Bring Back the Death Penalty. Bring Back the Police" and that "muggers and murderers . . . should be forced to suffer and, when they kill, they should be executed for their crimes."

⋮⋮⋮

But in 2002 Manhattan District Attorney Robert M. Morgenthau declared that the Central Park Five had not committed the crime and that charges would be dropped against all of them. DNA evidence had revealed that another man had alone perpetrated the rape. The young men were released from prison, having borne the agony of knowing they were innocent and victims themselves. Reporters and editors all but touched their chests apologetically over the years when confronted with their collective nonfeasance.

Some understandably felt that the Central Park Five case highlighted the tribulations of being Black and male in America. Heaven knows, our prisons holler mournful shrieks of agony, day and night, lonely and unheard, from tens of thousands of Black men, then and now. But the fact is that the episode made clear, more than anything, the still-surviving disregard for the lives and dignity of Black women.

⋮⋮⋮

Consider this.

Two weeks after Meili's rape, a thirty-nine-year-old Black woman in Brooklyn was savagely raped, sodomized, and thrown down the air shaft off a building's roof. Three men had seen the woman standing near a four-story building on Lincoln Place in Central Brooklyn. They grabbed her and pulled her into the building and then up to the roof, where they robbed her of her cash and jewelry before sexually assaulting her. The woman suffered life-threatening injuries and was still hospitalized a year later (in October of 1990), when her attackers were convicted and sentenced to terms of up to eighteen years in prison. Two of the men were arrested the day after the crime, and the third was caught two months later.

The depravity of the attack was almost as breathtaking as the paucity of media coverage. The relative inattention of the press sickened and angered a Brooklyn Pentecostal minister, the Rev. Herbert Daughtry, who drew at least some attention to the assault with press conferences in front of Kings County Hospital, where the victim had been taken right after the horrific assault. Rev. Daughtry was pastor of the House of the Lord Pentecostal Church in Downtown Brooklyn. (Even though Rev. Al Sharpton had spent part of his childhood on Lincoln Place, where the robbery and rape occurred, it was Daughtry, rather than Rev. Al, who bellowed continually about the racial disparities exposed to the world in that incident.)

"We say to all those who showed concern at Metropolitan Hospital to come here also," Daughtry said, referring to the hospital where Trisha Meili, the Central Park victim, was at the time. (That quote was in an article by reporter Charles Baillou, in the May 19, 1989, issue of the *Amsterdam News*, the Black weekly newspaper.)

At least one of those who had been making strong public statements denouncing the accused attackers of Trisha Meili took up the offer. That was realtor Donald Trump, who had been calling for the execution of the Black and Latino teens even before they were tried. Trump was reported in the *Amsterdam News* as having visited the Black woman, offering to pay some of her medical bills. Daughtry was quoted in the weekly paper as saying Trump was "trying to make up for the damage he's done."

(Note: Mainstream newspapers typically do not publish the names of the victims of sex crimes. However, the Central Park Five case became such a huge story that some outlets did use Trisha Meili's name in reports. Notable among these news outlets were the Black weekly *Amsterdam News*, the Brooklyn-based *City Sun*, and the Brooklyn-based *Daily Challenge*, all of which had Black readership.

Suffused in the reasoning of the Black editors, in using the victim's name, was the widely perceived notion among their readers that the victim was otherwise an example of white privilege that Blacks lived with for centuries and resented. Meili in the early 2000s eventually opened up publicly about her traumas and identified herself by name. On June 20, 2019, former *Daily Challenge* editor Dawad Wayne Philip wrote a reflection on the Central Park saga. He told readers that the story of Black male perpetrators and white female victims "has always been an historical and flammable red flag, from the deep south to New York City, from Emmett Till to the Scottsboro Boys, it is in the DNA of bloody American racism.")

Don Terry, a Black reporter then with the *New York Times*, wrote a May 29, 1989, article saying there had been twenty-eight other rapes or attempted rapes in New York City in the week overlapping the April 1989 attack on Meili. "Nearly all the rapes . . . were of black or Hispanic women," Terry reported, and they received little or no press attention.

Terry came up with summaries of sex assaults on Black and Latino women, day by day over a week during the month when Meili was attacked. (The *Times* began beefing up its local coverage in the mid- and late 1980s. It did so after, and because of, the entry of the well-financed *New York Newsday* onto the city's newspaper scene.)

In my years of reporting in New York City, one series of stories especially stands out for me. I wrote them in 1982 for the *New York Daily News*. The stories didn't earn me any prizes, national or local. I didn't even receive praise from my editors. In fact, I had to fight with editors even to get the stories in the paper; and when they did get published, they were on the back pages, in the regional section, called Manhattan/Bronx.

The victim of that story was a black Harlem barmaid, Shirley Grant, forty-two, who had been murdered by her jealous boyfriend. I had come upon the story because I'd been sitting in a West Harlem bar one evening, drinking, as I would do perhaps too much back then. (I was one of two reporters in a small *Daily News* Harlem bureau on West 125th Street.) Employees at the bar, the Mark IV bar on St. Nicholas Avenue, were talking with pain in their voices about the murdered woman they had loved so dearly. Her killing had not been reported by any newspaper or broadcast station. I was crushed by what I'd heard at the bar.

The next day I went right up to Grant's apartment in the Bronx, where she had been beaten to death with a lamp a few days before by a guy named Johnnie B. Johnson, fifty-one, a truck driver from Queens. She had been dating him but wanted to end the relationship, angering him.

I spoke with Grant's son and other family members. Back at my office, I called the Bronx district attorney and spoke with an assistant district attorney who asked me, with irritation, if I expected them to vigorously prosecute every single killing in the borough. I wrote stories. In reaction, Harlem City Councilman Frederick E. Samuel called me to say he and his community were outraged by the Bronx district attorney's attitude. Of course, I wrote another story, quoting him.

In reaction to that story, the Bronx district attorney, Mario Merola, called me to say his office would bring the boyfriend to justice and vigorously prosecute him. Johnnie Johnson was found on the run in Virginia and then brought back to New York, where he was put on trial, convicted, and sentenced to life in prison.

What stayed with me over the following months was a feeling among some *News* staffers that the Shirley Grant story was not worth the effort. For instance, the day I went to Grant's apartment in the

Bronx, I called the *News* to have a photographer assigned so we could have photos of Grant's son in her apartment. A newsroom source later told me that the photographer had returned and expressed puzzlement as to why he'd been sent out on such an insignificant story.

∷

As for Shirley Grant, the loving barmaid and mother, my contribution to justice for her was devoid of anguish on my part. It was surely nothing like the agonies experienced by journalist Jim DeRogatis, who struggled for years, decades later, to shine a light of attention on the Black-on-Black sex predations of rapper R. Kelly.

∷

The great Black intellectual and journalist W. E. B. Du Bois wrote in 1903, in his classic book *The Souls of Black Folk*, that Blacks live their lives behind a veil, maintaining a "double consciousness" that allows them to survive within themselves as well as in the racist society beyond. Pamela Newkirk aptly used that Du Bois analogy in her book *Within the Veil: Black Journalists, White Media*, published by New York University Press in 2000.

The book came out two years before it was revealed that the Central Park Five men had not raped the white investment bank worker. So Newkirk did not have the advantage of having the firm evidence of the racial double standard. But even so, she saw racism in the very extensive coverage of the attack on Trisha Meili.

"[I]f the Central Park jogger had been a black woman, even an affluent one, few believe that the media coverage would have been as prominent or as prolonged," wrote Newkirk.

After working at various news outlets, including two years at *New York Newsday* in the early 1990s, Newkirk went on to a life in academia, earning a doctorate and becoming a professor at New York University.

A Black woman who fought and survived for decades in the trenches of the white newspaper realm was Sheryl McCarthy. McCarthy worked as a reporter at the *New York Daily News* from 1977 to 1982 and later at *New York Newsday* for two decades.

After leaving *Newsday* in 2006, McCarthy began teaching at Queens College. In one of her courses, Journalism Ethics, she always began the semester with a study of the Central Park Five case. What did it show about society? About New York City? About journalism?

"We'd talk about how it became the biggest story in the city," McCarthy said, interviewed in 2020. "The journalists who covered that story fell for the template, that these were feral Black youths from Harlem who came down to our neighborhood to rape our women and steal our bicycles."

White newspapers gave up-front coverage to white women who were raped, regardless of the race of the assailant. But, other than the Brawley case, there were never daily stories about rapes of Black women. And it was not just the white media guilty of that dismissiveness, McCarthy said. Also blameworthy were Black men, including the Rev. Al Sharpton.

In 1995, McCarthy wrote a column expressing her anger that Sharpton and others in the Black community were planning to hold a parade celebrating the release from prison of professional boxer Mike Tyson, who had been convicted in Indiana in 1992 of raping an eighteen-year-old Black beauty pageant contestant.

"My feeling about Sharpton was that he could get outraged when he thought it was a situation of Black women being abused by white men, but not when it was a Black woman who was raped by a Black man, as with Mike Tyson," McCarthy said.

One of the other Black women who publicly criticized the plan to hold a parade for Tyson was Jill Nelson. Nelson had worked as a writer for the *Washington Post* from 1986 to 1990 and then wrote about her experiences at the *Post* in an acclaimed tell-all memoir, *Volunteer Slavery: My Authentic Negro Experience* (Penguin Books, 1994).

Nelson organized a march along West 125th Street in Harlem denouncing Sharpton and Black politicians who had agreed to honor Tyson, including Congressman Charles Rangel. In reaction, Tyson's admirers backed off their parade plans, but they continued to defend the boxer as someone they said was trying to make a change in his life.

The publisher of the *Amsterdam News*, the Black weekly paper, was one of those who strongly backed the idea of a celebration of Tyson's release from prison. On June 17, 1995, Wilbert (Bill) Tatum published a column strongly criticizing the protesters as Black puppets. Those who were protesting, including the *Newsday* columnist Sheryl McCarthy and journalist Jill Nelson, were doing so "due to the enormous pressure white media has exerted on you," Tatum wrote.

It was evident Tatum had not read Nelson's *Volunteer Slavery*, which was bold in exposing the macro- and micro-racism she had experienced as a writer for the *Washington Post*.

Newspapers Attempt Diversity, but Days Are Numbered

In their book *News for All the People: The Epic Story of Race and the American Media* (Verso Books, 2011), Juan González and Joseph Torres outline the white media's attempts to change their hiring policies during the last decades of the twentieth century.

In the early 1960s, almost no white newspaper had more than two Black reporters. The vast majority had none. But editors began to realize, after the racially turbulent decade of the '60s, that they needed to have reporters who could gain trust in Black communities. Newspapers were also under significant political pressures. That was especially so after the release in 1968 of the Kerner Commission Report. The commission attributed the nation's growing racial problems to segregation in education, housing, and journalism. It was especially harsh in criticizing white newspapers and other burgeoning forms of "the media."

"The press has too long basked in a white world looking out of it, if at all, with white men's eyes and white perspective," the commission wrote.

Prodded by the Kerner Report, the American Society of Newspaper Editors (ASNE) in 1972 conducted its "first ever" survey of newsroom diversity. "What it found was shocking," wrote authors González and Torres. "African-Americans comprised just 1 percent of personnel at the nation's daily newspapers—235 out of 23,111."

Six years later ASNE began conducting the first of what would be decennial surveys of diversity. Christopher Daly, in *Covering America: A Narrative History of a Nation's Journalism*, presents a small chart with the ASNE numbers over three decades. The chart shows how newspaper readership exploded after the 1960s but began to diminish toward the end of the century. And it reveals that minorities were seriously underrepresented, relative to their presence in the general population. In 1978 there were 43,000 newsroom jobs, of which 1,700 were minorities, or 3.95 percent; in 1988, 55,000 jobs, of which 3,900 were minorities, or 7.02 percent; in 1998, 54,700 jobs, of which 6,300 were minorities, or 11.46 percent; and in 2008, 52,600 jobs, of which 7,100 were minorities, or 13.52 percent.

Three significant patterns were developing over those years. One is that Latinos and Asians increasingly became lumped together with Blacks in the category of "minorities"; two, that growing numbers of educated minorities were making their voices heard and demanding significant presence in newsrooms, which showed itself in at least some increasing numbers; and, three, that ASNE as a society of newspaper administrators was becoming outdated. Cable, broadcast, and web news operations began overtaking newspapers as news conveyors.

ASNE stopped tallying newspaper jobs after the 2008 survey. Moreover, it changed its name from American Society of Newspaper Editors to American Society of News Editors in 2009, and then it merged with the Associated Press Media Editors, becoming the News Leaders Association.

By 2020 the number of newspapers and newspaper jobs had shrunk to the point of disappearing in some American markets. In 2020, Fordham University Press published *America's Last Great Newspaper War: The Death of Print in a Two-Tabloid Town*, a memoir by Mike Jaccarino, who had worked as a reporter at the *New York Post* and the *Daily News* in the twenty-first century.

In 2018, the Pew Research Center reported that the U.S. media (including newspapers and broadcast and Internet companies) remained strikingly white. About 77 percent of newsroom employees were "non-Hispanic" whites. The center also factored in gender, reporting that 61 percent of all news workers were males. The Pew Center is a nonprofit organization that does demographic research and media content analysis.

∷

In New York City of the 1990s, as Earl Caldwell exited the theater of white newspaper dramas, other Blacks were entering it; and they had roles in the playing out of the Sharpton saga.

One such journalist was Playthell Benjamin. Benjamin in the 1970s did public relations work for a boxing promoter. A gifted writer, he also read commentaries on radio station WBAI. The commentaries were thoughtful, well-crafted, and, indeed, intellectual. So impressed were editors of *The Village Voice*, New York City's popular alternative newspaper, that they reached out to Benjamin to see if he would write for them. He began publishing long articles for the Greenwich Village–based weekly.

Playthell Benjamin was a "truth-teller" in the vein of columnists at white daily tabloids, like Jimmy Breslin, Pete Hamill, and Les Payne. Among those who heaped strong praise on Benjamin were Mike Taibbi and Anna Sims-Phillips. They were the authors of *Unholy Alliances: Working the Tawana Brawley Story*, written during the thick of the Brawley episode.

In their book, the authors cited an Al Sharpton–bashing article Benjamin had written in July 1988 for *The Village Voice*. They called it a "brilliant analytical piece" and quoted from it. Referring to Sharpton, Benjamin had written: "The danger resides in his ability to excite the emotions of his black audiences and the irresponsible ends to which he uses this gift. His hyperbolic technique works like pouring salt into an open wound. . . ."

The piece was headlined "Jive at Five: How Big Al and the Bully-boys Bogarted the Movement." ("Bogart" was Black slang for taking over.) Benjamin's article ran 8,000 words, was cited by news observers, and launched Benjamin on a new path of recognition, even beyond America. After it ran in the *Voice*, the *Guardian* newspaper in Britain reached out to Benjamin and enticed him into doing articles for them. One of his first *Guardian* pieces, based on the *Voice* article, carried the headline, referring to Sharpton, "Hustler with a Charmed Life."

Then in about 1994 Benjamin began writing columns for the *Daily News*. He wrote on a range of people and topics, from the Latin American drug trade to the controversial Black Muslim leader Louis Farrakhan. But not about Rev. Al. In 1995, Benjamin says, the *News* nominated him for a Pulitzer Prize for commentaries. He left the paper after several years and began writing for alternative web outlets.

Now in his late seventies and retired from writing for publications, Playthell Benjamin looks on with astonishment at how Rev. Al has transformed himself into the effective leader of Black America in the third decade of the twenty-first century. (Unlike Rev. Al, Benjamin had been hunkered down during the 2020 months of the Covid-19 shutdown.)

In one of Benjamin's 2020 web commentaries, he wrote that Sharpton was historically unique in his efforts fighting injustices against Black Americans. He quoted from the eulogy Sharpton gave in Minneapolis in June 2020, after the video-recorded, knee-on-the-back murder of the Black man George Floyd by a white police officer. The web article bore the headline "God's Trombone Stirs Souls Around the World." (Benjamin has published his writings on his website at commentariesonthetimes.me.)

5

⬛⬛

Rev. Al, Wayne Barrett, and Old Black Brooklyn

THE REPORTER WHO most persistently hounded Al Sharpton throughout the minister's whole public life was Wayne Barrett of *The Village Voice*. Barrett threw print darts at Sharpton not just at the end of the 1980s and through the 1990s but well into the twenty-first century, after almost all others were lifting toasts to the Rev.

As a reporter and writer, Barrett incorporated the self-asserted virtues of journalism in New York City. Like many of the Irish columnists and reporters at the dailies, Barrett was raised in the Catholic faith. (Unlike most of the tabloid Irish reporters and editors, Barrett had actually studied for the priesthood. Although he left the seminary in the 1960s, the scholarly Jesuit training he received in his young adulthood stayed with him through his life, and he remained a devout Catholic until the end. His wife, Fran Barrett, informed me in a phone interview in 2020 that Wayne's mother was of Ukrainian descent and his father was of old *Mayflower* descent. She said, further, with an all-but-audible smile, that his love of the Irish played a starring role in his life, as in his young adult selection of a wife, Frances "Fran" McGettigan.)

Born in Connecticut and raised in Lynchburg, Virginia, Barret received his bachelor's from St. Joseph's University, a Jesuit institution in Philadelphia and then entered the seminary. Deciding to change his life course, he married and moved to New York City, where he entered the Columbia Graduate School of Journalism. Wayne Barrett and his lifelong partner, Fran, settled into the politically turbulent neighborhood of Brownsville, where Barrett became an activist. Brownsville is, meaningfully, where Sharpton lived in his childhood years. The place was full of political corruption and poverty, and there the lives of the two, Sharpton and Barrett, would overlap in the late 1970s.

It was a time when the white New York City newspapers were not paying much attention to Black neighborhoods and certainly not to the twentyish preacher Rev. Alfred Sharpton.

Wayne Barrett's relevance to the Sharpton story comes not just from his having attempted to expose each and every Sharpton misstep, blunder, and misstatement but from the lucidity and thoroughness of Barrett's reporting and writing, and from the perception of Barrett, within the broad journalism community and beyond, as committed to finding and telling the truth.

A defining distinction does exist, on the other hand, between Barrett and someone like Mike McAlary, Les Payne, and other daily newspaper journalists who wrote about Al Sharpton. Barrett was not in the frater-sorority of the city's daily newspaper reporters. He spent all of his reporting life with the alternative press, writing especially for the tabloid *Village Voice* weekly, whose origins lay in the hip West Village. It was said by many who knew Barrett that he could not have existed at a New York City daily tabloid newspaper. Those publications would have been, in so many ways, too confining for someone like Wayne Barrett, in the sense that they existed according to rigid rules of the craft of daily newspaper journalism, as it developed in the latter half of the twentieth century.

Daily newspaper stories, for the most part, were expected to be as brief as possible, with a simplicity that made a reader nod in acceptance and then perhaps take a breath of reflection. The stories were to be written in everyday English that gave a sense of strong schooling in rules of grammar but avoided multisyllabic words when shorter ones would make the point. The daily newspaper exception to those rules would have been the "Gray Lady" broadsheet, the *New York Times*. *Times* reporters were not writing as if they were "telling it to Sweeney."

Barrett had much of Sweeney in him, especially in his avowed populist political views. But his strong academic background showed itself in his researching and in his writing style. *Newsday* columnist and editor Les Payne once snarkily said that the *Voice* had a propensity to run investigative pieces that effectively said, "We've uncovered lots of people doing horrible things. Here are their names, addresses and the docket numbers of the cases." But Payne admired Wayne Barrett for his character and (perhaps mostly) for his willingness to withstand the rocks thrown at him after publication of exposés of wrongdoing by public figures. Public figures were fair game for Payne, Barrett, and other hard-nosed journalists. And, by the late 1980s, Sharpton had become, in the minds of every New York City journalist, regardless of writing style, a public figure.

Barrett's and Sharpton's First Encounters— 1970s Brownsville

Wayne Barrett crossed paths with the younger Alfred Sharpton in the late 1970s, when Sharpton was the boy preacher running all over the place with all kinds of ambitious politicians, activists, and entertainers. During this period, Rev. Al (or Rev. Alfred, as he was called before the '80s) was off the radar of the white press. Earl Caldwell acknowledged he had not heard of Sharpton before 1984 or so. And Payne, now deceased, would not have either, I'm fairly certain.

As a white guy who settled into a Black neighborhood in the 1970s, Barrett might be called one of the first "newcomers." That became the moniker used by Black Brooklynites in the twenty-first century, when they spoke of out-of-state whites who began moving into the gentrifying neighborhoods of Bedford-Stuyvesant, Bushwick, and other areas of the borough including, yes, Brownsville.

Often the "newcomers" are educated, ambitious, and eager to do good for those who have not had the advantages they've had. The same could have been said of Barrett. He settled into poor, crime-ridden Brownsville in the 1970s and developed the frame of mind (and the politics) that would guide his path over the remainder of his life.

Unlike mainstream journalists, Barrett did not shun close connections to politicians. The mainstreamers, at least in conversations with one another, almost always dismissed all politicians as self-serving and corrupt, perhaps by nature.

It so happened that at this point in Brooklyn's history, the 1970s, increasing numbers of elected officials and political wannabes were Black. Brooklyn was reaching its heights of Blackness, in terms of numbers and influence. The surge in the number of Blacks began after World War II, with the beginnings of the Great Migration from the South. That post–World War II wave included Alfred and Ada Sharpton (from Florida and Alabama, respectively). Their son Alfred was born at Kings County Hospital in 1954. Later in life, Sharpton would say that his birth in Brooklyn distinguished him, psychically, from Blacks who had come there after having been reared in the South. Those migrants (which included his parents) were more likely to have ingrained fears of whites, fears that came from personal experiences with officially sanctioned racial mistreatment.

By the 1970s Barrett and Sharpton began stepping (in respective ways) into the muck and mire of Brooklyn politics. (Barrett was in his thirties, Sharpton in his twenties.) Among the cadre of politically active Blacks back then was a rising cohort of educated Black men and women. Some had roots in the American South, and others came from relatively privileged backgrounds in the British Caribbean. In that latter group was Shirley Chisholm, who in 1968 became the first Black woman elected to Congress and who in 1972 made a well-publicized run for the American presidency. Teenager Alfred Sharpton, having come up in the Pentecostal Church, appealed to Shirley Chisholm for his natural speaking gifts and, certainly, for his root connections to the Black southerners in Brooklyn. Alfred Sharpton began accompanying Chisholm on campaign jaunts through the borough. (Though Chisholm has been portrayed, by herself and in documentaries, as a political radical, she was steeped in the local Democratic machine, which by the late 1970s was headed by the late, mob-connected Brooklyn Democratic boss Meade Esposito.)

As for Barrett, he began aligning with those politicians who today might be called local "progressives." Included in that group was a Black up-and-comer who was backed by Barrett and other whites with activist connections. That Black politician was Major Owens. Owens had migrated to Brooklyn from the South, having been born in Collierville, Tennessee, in 1936. He graduated from the historically Black Morehouse College in Atlanta, Georgia, and became a librarian.

Notably for that time and place, Owens's wife, Ethel Werfel Owens, was white; and he was otherwise also showing signs of what many hoped were coming social and political changes. Owens joined up with groups like CORE (the Congress of Racial Equality) and became a reliable fighter in the campaign against the Democratic Party machine. In 1974 he was elected to the state senate representing his Brownsville neighborhood. In 1978, he ran for reelection and a youngster named Alfred Sharpton, surprisingly to some, surfaced as a challenger. A problem for Sharpton arose when it was found out that he was registered to vote at two addresses, one being 390 Madison Street, and the other 1883 Bergen Street.

That disqualifying detail was discovered by none other than Wayne Barrett. And it seems that Barret found and disclosed this, not just because it was a good story, but rather because he was collaborating with Owens on various political projects in the community. Also, Barrett's wife, Fran Barrett, worked for Owens. She wrote proposals for community residents who operated day-care centers, a significant business in those days in Black Brooklyn.

The headlines that stemmed from the Sharpton vs. Owens episode were eye-opening for those who enjoyed the drama and intrigue of politics. (Because Sharpton was a decade from becoming the huge, attention-grabbing figure on the front pages of tabloids, his activities in Brooklyn at this time did not draw much attention in the white press. Barrett was just beginning his relationship with *The Village Voice*, and his articles were largely about mob and other corrupt influences on Brooklyn politics—including the maneuvers of realtor Fred Trump, father of Donald Trump.)

Sharpton's effort to get on the ballot against Owens had been backed by a Brownsville politician who had been working smugly in the system for more than a decade. Sam Wright had been a city council member representing the neighborhood. And in that very year of the Owens–Sharpton flare-up, 1978, Wright had been convicted of felony charges related to political corruption.

Even back then, at the young age of twenty-three, Sharpton was smooth. He denied to the press that he had any unlawful intentions in being registered at two addresses. "I had registered at the Madison Street address where I had an office. The office was moved and I then registered at my home address on Bergen Street in June and because I was not living there for a year I cannot run," Sharpton was quoted as saying in the September 7, 1978, edition of the *Amsterdam News*. (The Black-owned *Amsterdam* weekly newspaper was based in Harlem but during its decades-long history also had offices in Brooklyn.)

Someone with knowledge of the future—when Sharpton was discovered in 1988 to have been using a bugged telephone to record conversations with unsuspecting callers—might have chuckled at one part of that 1978 Owens–Sharpton story.

It turned out that Sharpton had secretly recorded a telephone conversation with Owens. Sharpton then declared publicly that the recording had revealed Owens had offered Sharpton a job if he pulled out of the campaign against Owens. Reacting to what Sharpton said, Owens countered that it was, first of all, shocking that Sharpton had recorded their conversation without Owens's approval and, second, that anyone listening to the exchange would note that Sharpton was trying to see if Owens would let Sharpton get a paid position working with a neighborhood group for youngsters.

The *Amsterdam* newspaper itself became so disgusted with what was going on that its editors published a statement saying, "The Amsterdam News will not print anymore of the controversy between Sen. Owens and the Rev. Sharpton because we feel that our space is much more valuable, in that it can be used for information supporting our communities."

Sharpton had to give up that attempt to unseat Owens, and Owens declared that his lawyers were looking into whether Sharpton had violated the law in recording someone without prior consent of the recorded party.

Owens won the primary and the general election.

Barrett retained within himself, beginning in those days, a feeling of Sharpton as an untrustworthy hustler, one representing the worst traits in politicians. As Sharpton grew in his abilities to make amends with journalists, he would generally return Barrett's phone calls and chat with him amicably. But Barrett continued to shoot hot printer's ink at Sharpton, even decades later.

"Man of Too Many Parts"

Moving forward to 1982, Sharpton was all over the place—in Brooklyn, on the road with James Brown, hustling to intimidate white music producers into using more Blacks, working tirelessly, though without serious financial accounting records. This was all fitting for a man of too many parts. ("Man of Too Many Parts" was the headline of an article in *The New Yorker*, written in 1993 by Jim Sleeper, who during the 1980s and '90s also did columns for *The Village Voice*, *New York Newsday*, and the *New York Daily News*.) In 1982, Sharpton was still making rounds in Brooklyn, but he had also been traveling the world and country with his stand-in father-figure, "Godfather of Soul" singer James Brown. Sharpton had also gotten to know and do business with boxing promoter Don King. But a bit of old-fashioned Black Brooklyn politics was still in Sharpton's blood.

Brooklyn, at that moment in 1982, was readying itself for congressional races that were to change the face of the borough, that is to say, the color of the faces of its congressmembers. Because of growing consciousness of the need for more racial diversity among Brooklyn's elected representatives, the state legislature in Albany had to redraw the lines of congressional districts. Those changes are based on the decennial census. In this instance it took place in 1980.

Essentially, on a more limited and emergency scale, the legislature had done something similar in the late 1960s. That was when it redrew central Brooklyn's congressional lines leading to Shirley Chisholm's victory and the emergence of Brooklyn's first Black member of Congress and America's first Black female member of Congress. But even after Chisholm's election, Blacks were complaining that state legislators in Albany were continuing to "gerrymander" congressional district lines, so that white voters would predominate and white congressmembers would stay in office. Angry Black voices were heard in Albany. And so 1982 became a signal moment.

The legislature made district line changes so that two Blacks would likely become members of Congress. This would help to make Black Brooklyn the Black American political powerhouse it would become by the end of the twentieth century, far outdistancing Harlem in population and number of Black elected officials.

And Rev. Al Sharpton was to play a role in it.

After Shirley Chisholm bowed out and retired from politics in 1982, a significant part of her newly drawn district fell into the eastern Brooklyn province where Edolphus Towns was the Democratic machine preference. Like Sharpton, Towns saw in local politics a reflection of the Black character as it evolved from the American South. Like Rev. Al, he came up in the Pentecostal Church and later became a Baptist.

Towns, born in Chadbourn, North Carolina, was backed by the Brooklyn Democratic machine, including the part headed by Wesley McDonald Holder, the early-twentieth-century immigrant from Guyana who was Shirley Chisholm's Brooklyn manager during her tenure in Congress.

With the hearty approval of the Brooklyn Democratic bosses, Towns selected young Alfred Sharpton to help him in his campaign for Congress. (Towns had been a Democratic district leader and Brooklyn Deputy Borough President in the 1970s.) Towns had nothing but praise for Sharpton as a political booster. "He could talk, and we used him as much as we could," Towns recalled, referring to the appearances Sharpton made at churches and other venues on Towns's behalf. "He could be riveting, and he chose the right words all the time. He benefited us greatly."

Towns won the primary handily with a substantial plurality of the vote and then went on to win the general election against the Republican, as was expected.

But over there in the newly drawn neighboring congressional district, covering Brownsville and parts of what today is East Flatbush, things were not quite as smooth.

A Black Brownsville politician named Vander Beatty entered the race for that newly drawn district. He was competing against Major Owens. Owens had the backing of the borough's progressives, the ones being lauded by *Village Voice*–reading left-wingers and an emerging group of Black nationalist–leaning activists such as Al Vann, who were also considered "anti-machine."

Beatty had the backing of the machine. Like so many others in Black Brooklyn, Beatty had arrived from the South. He had earned a bachelor's degree from Johnson C. Smith University, an historically Black college in Charlotte, North Carolina. There at Johnson C. Smith, he had pledged the Kappa Alpha Psi fraternity, which prided itself on having many members who were becoming teachers, lawyers, and successful businessmen. The fraternity also had a reputation for throwing fired-up parties, where guys and gals bopped to the beat of the latest R&B songs and pumped fists in the air.

Beatty jumped into Black Brooklyn's politics game and got into the orbit of Sam Wright, the Black Democratic machine politician. With Wright's backing, Beatty won election to the New York Assembly in the early 1970s and then went on to win a seat in the New York Senate.

In 1982 things went from bad to worse in Black Brooklyn politics, and, again, Sharpton was involved.

Prosecutors gathered evidence showing that Vander Beatty had hacked out a scheme related to his primary race against Owens. Owens had won a majority of the votes. But investigators—among them journalist/activist Wayne Barrett, Owens's friend and ally—uncovered evidence that Beatty supporters had sneaked into Board of Elections locations to secretly create false registration cards. The intent was to have the cards be used as evidence of fraud—and thereby a need for an official recounting of the vote that had resulted in Owens's victory.

Witnesses and evidence were gathered by Brooklyn's district attorney, Elizabeth Holtzman. Beatty was arrested and charged with fraud.

No one said that Al Sharpton was among those who entered the Board of Elections after hours at night or that he tinkered with voter registration cards or created false ones. The finger-pointing regarding Sharpton had to do with the young minister/activist's supposed close relationship with Beatty. As the young minister did with Towns in Towns's race for Congress, Sharpton appeared with Vander Beatty during the campaign season. Notably, on the steps of City Hall, Sharpton and Beatty held a joint press conference that was mentioned in the *New York Times*. (The two called for a cutoff of federal funds to New York City public schools until the school system complied with U.S. efforts to get the city to improve the racial balance among city teachers and education administrators. The Beatty/Sharpton press conference was reported in the June 5, 1982, issue of the *New York Times*, with an article headlined "Call Made for U.S. to End School Aid.")

Unbent by what had happened to him, Beatty in the courtroom denounced the whole process as a sham of justice and an example of crude political race targeting. At his 1984 sentencing, the *New York Times* quoted Beatty as saying to the court that "there's not one white elected official in the state" who would have been put on trial based on what prosecutors had. It happened to him, he said, because he was "a black nigger." ("Beatty Is Given 16 Months for Election Fraud," Joseph P. Fried, *New York Times*, February 4, 1984.)

Beatty would face other corruption charges and guilty verdicts, sending him to state prisons through the remainder of the decade. He asked at one point for a relocation to another upstate facility, citing assaults against him. When he was finally released in 1990, even then still unbowed, he announced that he would be making a political comeback and was preparing to run in a local race.

However, while in his office on Sterling Place, between Crown Heights and Prospect Heights, a gunman walked in and shot him to death. It was weeks later before a suspect was finally apprehended, on the run, in Chicago. A reason for the shooting, it was speculated at the time, was that the suspect, Arthur E. Flournoy, a retired New York City Corrections Department captain and friend of Beatty's, was upset over a past dealing with Beatty. Beatty had supposedly recommended to him a lawyer in a matter involving Flournoy's estranged wife. But Flournoy became very upset with the way the lawyer was handling the matter and directed his anger at Beatty. (That account was in a *New York Times* story of January 14, 1993.)

A jury ultimately acquitted Flournoy of the murder. Representing Flournoy then was an attorney he was obviously very pleased with. That lawyer was Michael W. Warren, the Black lawyer with Black nationalist/leftist leanings who represented many Black victims of police violence in the 1980s and '90s. Warren had made the case that there was insufficient evidence that Flournoy had been in Beatty's office that day.

Beatty's family was obviously crushed by the whole matter. They did not want to speak with me after I reached out to them in 2020. I had told them I'd take notes only if they felt it would help them heal. What seemed clear was that Beatty's surviving nuclear family had acquired a strong distaste for politics, especially the Brooklyn variety.

###

Beatty's is one of the saddest stories in postmodern Black Brooklyn political history. Recently I went to the address where Beatty was gunned down in his office. Newspapers reported it as being 457 Sterling Place. Because of changes made to building structures in the vicinity, that address no longer exists and it does not show up in New York City property tax searches. Except to his family and those still living who were involved in politics at that time, Beatty is a forgotten figure.

A fact known and shared with me by political insiders in Black Brooklyn was that Beatty had been raped while he was in prison. (That would be consistent with his reported efforts to be removed from one prison locale to another, citing abuse.)

Many of the politicians involved in those political clashes with Sharpton then are dead now. But today, there still exists in Brooklyn some bitterness against Sharpton for what happened in the old political arena.

There is lingering resentment in the mind and voice of a son of Major Owens regarding the clashes between his father and Rev. Al in the old days.

Major Owens stayed in Congress from 1983 until 2007. When he stepped down, one of the contenders in the extremely bitter battle to replace him was his son Chris Owens. Chris Owens was unsuccessful, and the seat eventually went to Yvette Clarke, daughter of former Council Member Una Clarke. Una Clarke, today a member of the CUNY (City University of New York) Board of Trustees, was active in Central Brooklyn politics in the 1970s and '80s, as Major Owens was making his way up the political ladder with Sharpton as his thorn. Major Owens died in 2013.

Major's son Chris says his dad was a standout example of the good that politicians can do and have done in Brooklyn.

Chris Owens holds a bachelor's degree from Harvard and a master's in Public Affairs and Urban and Regional Planning from Princeton. In 2020 he was Chief of the Re-Entry Bureau at the Office of the Brooklyn District Attorney.

Anger comes across in his voice as he speaks of Sharpton. Still strong in his memory is the 1978 tale of Sharpton's tape-recording a call with Major Owens and then later accusing Major Owens of offering the minister a bribe. The reports were talked about all over Black Brooklyn and beyond. Chris Owens said, speaking to me in the summer of 2020: "I was nineteen and I was working at a law firm and I saw this. I was crying . . . . When the *Amsterdam News* board heard the tape, they realized there was nothing there [of substance]. That's when I first saw Sharpton [for who he was]."

He added, "My father's take was that he was a ho [whore], that Sharpton basically understood how to shake people down. . . . What always puzzled me was, first, the fact that Sharpton always had money. How was he funded?" One person involved in Black Brooklyn politics in those days said the following to me in 2020: that some of the players in Central Brooklyn machine politics back then were "bag men," with off-the-books payments. Sharpton has consistently denied taking illicit money from politicians.

Chris Owens's assertions of Sharpton's "shaking people down" come, in good part, from reports in the early '80s that Sharpton pressured some businesses and big entertainment venues to contribute to his National Youth Movement or, implicitly, face massive protests against them.

Owens maintains that Sharpton's attempts at political office—the runs for a U.S. Senate seat in 1992 and 1994; for New York City mayor in 1997; and for president in 2004—were all "efforts to build himself as a powerbroker, not to get a job that would allow him to make legal and administrative changes."

He said, "Sharpton never ran for an office he could win . . . . Sharpton didn't want the responsibility, for governing. He learned that he could make money, do what he liked to do, and become very well known, without the responsibilities."

Among Chris Owens's heroes from the 1970s and beyond was journalist Wayne Barrett, the one who had raised alarms in 1978 about Sharpton's being registered to vote at more than one address, the same Barrett who would hound Sharpton throughout Barrett's life as a reporter/activist.

There are others today who oppose what Sharpton was doing in Brooklyn politics in the late 1970s but say they see and appreciate his rise and perceived changes.

Maurice Reid managed Major Owens's campaign for Congress in 1982 and served as Owens's chief of staff during the congressman's successive years in office. Reid told me by telephone in 2020 that he harbors no resentments at all toward Sharpton. He said he appreciates the work Sharpton's been doing in his transformative years. Reid also affirmed that in the 1970s and early '80s Sharpton was clearly in the camp of the Brooklyn machine, meaning Meade Esposito, Sam Wright, and Vander Beatty (all three of whom went on to be convicted of crimes related to abuses of political power).

"Wright, Beatty, Al, they were all opposed to what we were talking about and what Major represented," Reid said. At the time of the phone interview with Reid, he was seventy-nine and, while technically retired, doing volunteer work with community groups, especially those connected with his beloved Brownsville neighborhood.

Reid was firm in stating that even Shirley Chisholm, so beloved for battling national politicians for their sexism, was operating with the Brooklyn Democratic machine during her years in Congress.

Reid said that Shirley Chisholm left her local political decisions to her manager, Wesley McDonald Holder, who was tied in strongly with the machine. "As long as she [Chisholm] got elected, she went along with Holder," he said, adding that, yes, "Mac Holder clearly was supporting Vander Beatty," the perpetrator of the electoral forgeries uncovered in 1982.

Inner Racial Animus Underlies Conflicts

Al Sharpton's base of support, when he became a huge name in the mid- and late 1980s, following Howard Beach and Tawana Brawley, was almost totally in the Black community. But race—that is to say, the proud embracing of one's Blackness—was a factor during the 1970s also. And Owens, though very progressive, was not seen as a "race man." Quite the opposite. Many Blacks did not react with gut enthusiasm regarding Owens's connections to white progressives (or his white wife).

Clearly, a singular focus on race did not drive the majority of Blacks in Owens's Central Brooklyn district. He got re-elected over and over again and served in Congress for twenty-four years. Still, many Blacks were sensitive about white involvement that they deemed to be intrusive.

"Major Owens and company, we used to call them integrationists," Waldaba Stewart, at this writing eighty-four years old, said. "They [Owens's crowd] were concerned about getting along with white people. I didn't care whether white people thought well of me or not. My interest was my people first." Stewart served four years in the state senate, representing his Central Brooklyn district (roughly Crown Heights and eastward toward Brownsville). He was challenged and defeated by machine candidate Vander Beatty in 1972.

Though not aligned politically with Stewart in the 1980s, Sharpton indicated that he shared Stewart's concerns about white liberal intrusion into Black affairs back then. Sharpton saw the whites who were opposed to his favored Black local politicians as interlopers, the term used by Blacks for white newcomers in the gentrification era of the twenty-first century. At the top of the list of interlopers back in the 1970s, by Sharpton's account, were Wayne Barrett and Jack Newfield.

Barrett and Newfield began teaming up at *The Village Voice*, and they showed clear, muscular support for Owens and against the hated Democratic machine. And in doing so they didn't have to show pretenses of "objectivity" that reined in the personal biases of reporters at the daily newspapers in New York City.

Sharpton said those whites who were teamed up with Owens often very unfairly castigated the Black Democratic machine politicians. "Y'all put Sam Wright in jail and brag about it, you put Vander Beatty in jail and brag about it," Sharpton said.

(Of interest is that while Barrett was an upper-class white Catholic liberal interloper from Virginia, Jack Newfield was born and raised in the Bedford-Stuyvesant section of Brooklyn. He graduated from Boys High School, the same school my dad and his two brothers graduated from in the late 1930s and early 1940s.)

6

Enter James Brown and Don King

THE ENTRANCE OF the "Godfather of Soul" James Brown into Sharpton's life is also tied into Brooklyn politics. It's a representation of the "six degrees of separation" concept that Black people often use to describe lifelong relationships that developed seemingly by chance.

In 1971, with the help of Brooklyn Congresswoman Shirley Chisholm, the boy preacher Rev. Alfred would start the National Youth Movement. The NYM would be the source of his popularity with many, and it was also a reason why politicians wanted to connect with him. Among the politicians who worked with Sharpton, putting together the paperwork for the National Youth Movement, were David Dinkins, the Harlem-based attorney who in 1990 would become New York City's first Black mayor; Percy Sutton, who would go on to become Manhattan Borough President and a candidate for mayor; and Clarence Jones, one of the owners of the *Amsterdam News*, the premiere Black newspaper in New York City. (Note: Improper handling of the NYM's finances would later lead to legal problems for Sharpton, and embarrassment for mayoral candidate Dinkins, but Sharpton was never found guilty of improprieties related to it.)

According to Sharpton's telling, one of the early members of his new youth group was a nineteen-year-old Black man with ambitions to become a lawyer. "[He] came up from Georgia wanting to go to Columbia Law School," Sharpton recalled, speaking in 2020. "He joined my youth group and we found out he was James Brown's son."

Teddy Brown—the "Godfather of Soul's" son—and two friends were soon thereafter, in 1973, killed in a car accident in upstate New York. Sharpton said James Brown was devastated by the tragedy and wanted to have a large celebration of his son's life. But the "Godfather," in Sharpton's telling, was nervous because he had begun to receive blowback from militant Blacks who were enraged that Brown had endorsed right-wing Republican President Richard Nixon. That was in 1972, when Nixon was running for reelection. The Godfather wanted to avoid sponsoring any event that might draw Blacks who would protest against him.

The solution? "He [James Brown] called [New York radio personality] Hank Spann and said, 'Mr. Spann, I'd like to do something for Teddy, but I don't want to deal with them picketers,'" Sharpton recalled.

(Spann helped promote singers by making sure their pop songs were played at popular hours on his WWRL-AM radio show. Spann was becoming enormously popular as the voice of pop radio. The station was owned by Egmont Sonderling, owner of Sonderling Broadcasting. Sonderling was white but had stations around the country specializing in Black music and topics.)

Spann then reached out to Bob Law, who was doing community outreach for the station. Speaking to me in 2020 by phone, Law recalled, "I told Spann, 'I know this young little preacher in Brooklyn that I've known for a while. He has a Black youth initiative. I said he's the first one who comes to mind. So I took [James Brown] to Alfred, and that was it.'"

Law continued, "James Brown . . . wanted to identify with a Black organization working on behalf of young Black people in particular. James had no connections with people in the street. He wanted to be identified with a kind of freedom movement and a youth empowerment movement. He felt this would help him. People were upset with him for his political choices."

As a result of Law's intervention, Brown did a big show on August 17, 1973, at the old RKO Albee Theater in Downtown Brooklyn. (The RKO Albee later became the Albee Square Mall.) The Brooklyn event pulled in $25,000 in gross ticket sales, with 10 percent going to the National Youth Movement, Sharpton said. Brown would also perform on behalf of the National Youth Movement at Madison Square Garden on July 4, 1974, and '75. The Madison Square Garden performances earned a gross total of $40,000 to $50,000, with the same 10 percent going to the NYM, Sharpton said.

Regarding Brown's decision in 1972 to go to the White House to meet with Nixon, Law chuckled, saying James Brown "would have gone to the White House of whoever invited him."

The relationship between the soul singer and the boy preacher would last through Brown's next three decades, until his death in Georgia in 2006. Brown would do concerts and make money, a bit of which flowed to Sharpton and youngsters working with him. Critics would say that Sharpton misused his organization, the National Youth Movement; and he was later accused of providing tickets to organized hustlers who allegedly used them for "scalping" (i.e., selling tickets at higher prices and making unreported profits). None of those accusations against Sharpton ever stuck.

Sharpton traveled extensively with Brown, and it was because of Brown that he began "conking" his hair, having it woven into that chemically slicked, straightened style used by James Brown, Little Richard, and other Black performers. The emerging cadre of Black nationalists in New York frowned upon "hair processing," because they said it was like trying to "become white" in physical appearance. Sharpton said the Godfather made him vow to keep his James Brown conk.

(In the 2000s, as he soared to national fame and influence, Sharpton lost his fat, going from 300 pounds to 130, through rigid dieting; and he gave up the track suits that would flop over his bulging torso and his back. But while he abandoned the wild, greased-back James Brown look, he retained the hair slickness that still suggested a professional coiffure. By the second decade of the twenty-first century, it was that new Sharpton, in conservative suits, who would be seen on cable news and at pulpits giving nationally televised eulogies for Black men killed by whites.)

In the 1970s, Rev. Alfred was budding. Emerging. And he was doing so with James Brown.

In books he would publish later in life, Sharpton would open up about childhood traumas, especially his father's deserting the household in the 1960s, when the Rev. was still a child. The Rev.'s stand-in father figure, James Brown, was also dealing with inner Freudian traumas that he never opened up much about. Later biographies and documentaries showed how he had experienced childhood stresses of his own. His mother had left him when he was four years old, and he spent part of his childhood living in a brothel managed by an aunt in Georgia.

But both Sharpton and Brown displayed an inner ability to bounce back from adversity. And Brown, the elder, would constantly pass along words of wisdom to Sharpton during their travels: Be who you are; show your pride. One piece of Black wisdom was bellowed in the title of a 2016 Brown biography, written by a renowned Black journalist and novelist, James McBride. The book was *Kill 'em and Leave* (Penguin Random House).

Don King, Big Trouble

Sharpton has said it was during his time in Zaire, Africa, with James Brown, in 1974, that he met Don King. Sharpton was traveling with

Brown as a kind of promoter. According to Sharpton in his 1996 auto-biography *Go and Tell Pharaoh*, the president of Zaire, Joseph Mobuto, wanted to have a big-name performer at the boxing match that the world was paying attention to—the fight between Muhammad Ali and George Foreman, known as "The Rumble in the Jungle." In his book, Sharpton writes that Mobutu had said the only Black Americans he had previously ever heard of were Muhammad Ali and James Brown. There in Zaire also with those big-name Americans was the money-making fight promoter Don King. (Note: Zaire today is officially known as the Democratic Republic of the Congo.)

The relationship that Sharpton was to develop with King was not on the order of the one with James Brown, but Don King was going to have an effect on Sharpton's life—recorded, as it were, in Sharpton's 1983 sit-down with federal investigators.

The journalist who shined a light that would make Don King, literally, well known as a killer and associate of organized-crime figures was Jack Newfield, the *Village Voice* reporter and pal of Sharpton's would-be nemesis Wayne Barrett. Newfield wrote a biography of Don King titled *The Life and Crimes of Don King: The Shame of Boxing in America* (Harbor Electronic Publishing, 2003).

In the beginning of his book, Newfield lays out the gruesome details that made King a kind of reflection of the Black folk villain "Stagger Lee." Stagger Lee entered the popular mind in the late 1950s, thanks to Lloyd Price's recording of the folk song about him that rose to the top of the pop R&B charts. After a dispute over who won as they were "shooting dice," Stagger Lee fired a pistol at his rival "Billy," even as Billy pleaded for his life:

> "Stagger Lee," cried Billy
> "Oh, please don't take my life.
> I got three little children
> And a very sickly wife."

Don King brought that folk narrative back to life, as it were. Newfield reported—using old court documents and clips from Cleveland, Ohio, newspapers, in addition to other secondary sources—that Don

King in April 1966 got into an angry verbal exchange with a man named Sam Garrett. Garrett had lost to King in a "numbers" bet and did not pay King $600 that Garrett owed him from the loss. Though King was 106 pounds heavier than Garrett—and Garrett was a sickly drug user—King kicked him over and over again. Many witnesses were on the scene. King was holding an unlicensed gun, while Garrett was unarmed. "Don, I'll pay you the money," Garrett was heard saying before he passed out, to die in a hospital five days later. King was eventually found guilty of second-degree murder and served four years in prison. (He was pardoned in 1983 by Republican Ohio Governor James Rhodes.)

Upon release from prison, King used connections from his earlier life, as a hustler with mob ties, to move on and become a big-time boxing promoter. It was both interesting and poetic that one of the R&B singers who helped King organize his "Rumble in the Jungle" boxing match in Zaire in 1974 was Lloyd Price—the same Price whose hit song "Stagger Lee" mirrored King's murder of the frail, pleading man who didn't have the money to pay King for a bet the man had lost.

⁝⁝

Sharpton says that during his secret 1983 meetings with FBI agents, the Feds were mostly trying to get Sharpton to find incriminating evidence regarding Don King. They had been attempting for several years to build a prosecutable case against King, regarding his known ties to organized crime and the overlap between the gangsters and professional boxing. They scared Sharpton into cooperating with them by threatening him with drug charges for which agents later admitted they did not have evidence. They also got Sharpton to agree to help get information leading to prosecutions of Italian American mobsters. Some of those associations came via Sharpton's work with

Blacks in the music industry. But Sharpton had also developed shady relationships with gangsters as he tried to pressure companies—including a private garbage collection business—to hire youth from the Black community. (Much of this was in the February 2, 1988, *Village Voice* article that followed the January 20, 1988, blockbuster *Newsday* exposé about Sharpton.)

Sharpton said to me that the Feds were even attempting to link King with Black nationalists. "Part of their thing was that Don King was giving money to the Black Liberation Army [so that he could] . . . get muscle when boxers got out of line or the mob tried to [interfere with his work]," Sharpton said in one interview. One other thing they also requested, which Sharpton doesn't easily talk about, was that he help locate fugitive Black revolutionaries.

FBI sources later told reporters that Sharpton did not come up with anything usable against King. He did, however, help the Feds get information that enabled them to trail mobster Federico "Fritzy" Giovanelli and successfully prosecute him for racketeering, according to mob reporter William Bastone.

In interviews with me, Sharpton has said the only things he was trying to do with the Feds was turn over hurtful information about drug traffickers' inflicting harm on Black communities and come up with incriminating facts about whites who were stealing money from Black music artists and producers.

Sharpton has strenuously maintained he'd never had links with Black revolutionaries and never had intentions of having them captured by the Feds. There were many then, as there are still some today, who don't accept that Sharpton's activities for the Feds were as limited as he maintains.

Losing the Black Nationalists

The 1983 meetings between Sharpton and the federal agents, as revealed by *New York Newsday* in January 1988, shook the Black Nationalist community in New York.

Perhaps chief among those who said they felt betrayed was Viola Plummer.

Thin, dark-complexioned, feisty, and gruff in manner, Plummer had been associated with a group of Black revolutionaries in New York City and was one of the "New York Eight," who were arrested and jailed in the early 1980s for allegedly helping convicted Black nationalists escape capture and detention. She and the others were acquitted.

The newspaper revelation of Sharpton's work with the Feds infuriated Plummer and her companions, though they had all along harbored suspicions about the minister's motives in his activism. Plummer revealed her revulsion toward Rev. Al at a public gathering.

Speaking at a Harlem meeting of activists in November 1992, held to discuss the legacy of assassinated Black leader Malcolm X, Plummer was quoted in the *Amsterdam News.* "We must defend Malcolm, by telling the truth to the people. You can't walk on both sides of the street and tell the truth. If you know that Al Sharpton is the police and don't tell it to the people—you're not telling the truth, you're not defending Malcolm!" (*Amsterdam News,* "Harlem Forum of Activists Discuss Malcolm X Legacy," by Akinshiju C. Ola, November 21, 1992).

Another close associate of Plummer's, Coltrane Chimurenga, was quoted in 1988 by the *Amsterdam News* as saying he and colleagues had done their own "internal investigation" and determined that Sharpton was a "traitor" (*Amsterdam News,* "Leaders Deny Rift in Outrage," by Jesse H. Walker, June 25, 1988). Chimurenga died in 2019.

Before the January 1988 exposé broke, Plummer, Chimurenga, and other Black revolutionaries had been guardedly working along with Sharpton during the Tawana Brawley and other protests. They did so as part of the protest group called the December 12 Movement. December 12, 1987, was the day when they had planned to conduct mass demonstrations showing concern for Tawana Brawley (still widely believed at that point to have been raped by white law-enforcement officers). Members of the group have said, speaking back then, that Sharpton had not been part of those original plans but had inserted himself. After the disclosure, just a month later, of Sharpton's links with Feds, group members asserted Sharpton had effectively "bogarted" (taken over) the movement.

Efforts to reach Plummer in 2020 were not successful, despite calls to associates of hers. (One of them told me explicitly, speaking off the record, that I should not try to interview her.)

Sharpton himself acknowledged that his ties with New York Black nationalists were conflicted. He said he believes he has been an unfair victim of some of their past statements.

Speaking of Viola Plummer and Coltrane Chimurenga, Sharpton said: "They put out there this bogus story that I'm disrupting the movement, that I'm an agent. [But] how long could you [say] that when I'm the one doing the next [protest march], in Bensonhurst [where he protested the killing by whites there of a Black man, Yusuf Hawkins] . . . Viola and them [sic] didn't do that. I did. And then the next case and the next case and the next case. It wasn't like they were out there doing anything. They went and got government jobs." (Over recent decades Plummer had worked with Charles Barron, who represented the Brownsville section of Brooklyn in the city council and then in the state assembly.)

Sharpton said that in the early 1990s he tried to mend relations with the Black nationalists. He said that he, Plummer, and others met at the Queens home of Sonny Carson. (Carson had been one of my sources when I wrote my 1988 story about Sharpton's working with federal agents who were trying to locate fugitive Black revolutionary Assata Shakur.) Carson had gained much derision in the white press once for saying publicly that he shouldn't be called anti-Semitic because "I don't just hate Jews. I hate all white people."

Sharpton said that as a result of that sit-down at Carson's home an understanding was reached, although clearly the nationalists did not affirm any lasting trust of Sharpton. "We all kind of agreed that we disagreed but would work together as much as we could," Sharpton said.

The Mob

One of the journalists who stayed on Sharpton's trail past the 1990s was William Bastone. Bastone had worked once for *The Village Voice* but then went on to obtain funding for a project called "The Smoking Gun." The "Smoking Gun" used the Freedom of Information Act to make so-called FOIA requests and obtain materials about organized-crime figures.

In 2014, Bastone released a trove of documents from Sharpton's 1983 meetings with federal agents, who got Sharpton to bug conversations with gangsters and assorted other crime suspects. One set of "bugs," Bastone wrote, had to do with organized crime member Federico "Fritzy" Giovanelli. Giovanelli had links to the old Brooklyn Democratic organization when it was led by Meade Esposito, and he had ties also to the "payola" scandal involving entertainers and radio stations. He therefore overlapped a bit with the young Sharpton, whose activities and relationships back then were associated with entertainers, radio stations, and Brooklyn machine politicians.

Bastone wrote that federal investigators used information gathered from Sharpton to apply for warrants to tap Giovanelli's phone. Giovanelli was a Genovese Mafia soldier. As Bastone reported, Giovanelli was sentenced to twenty years in prison for racketeering "following a trial during which those recordings were played for jurors."

Bastone quoted Giovanelli as saying in 2014 that Sharpton had come a long way from the man he was in the early 1980s, and the past should remain the past. "Poor Sharpton, he cleaned up his life and you want to ruin him," Giovanelli was quoted as saying, while laughing. Giovanelli was eighty-two and had been released from federal prison several years before. He died in 2018.

Barrett Passes on, Sharpton Absent

Wayne Barrett used to tell his interns that journalists were detectives for the people. Over the course of three decades he tutored, and badgered, hundreds of interns, who labored for free. In tributes before and after Barrett's death, many of them testified to having gained immeasurable journalistic riches from him. Barrett, for them, epitomized the craft of journalism as the searching for and the telling of truth.

Barrett, in his reporting, had found hidden details about mob-connected Brooklyn and its connections to real estate barons, perhaps the most significant of them being Fred Trump (along with his son Donald).

Barrett wrote about Donald Trump in *Village Voice* articles and then in a book that would have wide ramifications: *Trump: The Deals and the Downfall*, published by HarperCollins in 1992. The book was updated and re-published in 2016 with the title *Trump: The Greatest Show on Earth: The Deals, the Downfall, the Reinvention.* In late 2016, when Trump was elected president of the United States, countless journalists from around the world flocked to Barrett's house in Brooklyn, where he kept reams of materials from his reporting days, to ask him questions and benefit from his generosity and informed knowledge of Trump's misdeeds.

Barrett died after a long battle with interstitial lung disease, his death occurring on January 19, 2017—the night before Trump was inaugurated as the forty-fifth president of the United States.

In September 2020, friends, former colleagues and interns who continued to mourn Barrett, three years after his death, celebrated the publishing of a book that paid tribute to his character and life's work. It was titled *Without Compromise: The Brave Journalism That First Exposed Donald Trump, Rudy Giuliani, and the American Epidemic of Corruption*, published by Bold Type Books in Manhattan. It carried the late Wayne Barrett's name as author, with Eileen Markey as editor. Markey was a former intern of Barrett's and in 2020 was a professor of journalism at Lehman College in the Bronx.

In some ways, regarding Rev. Al Sharpton, Wayne Barrett died a lonely man. Virtually every reporter in the mainstream (as well as white alternative) media greatly respected Barrett for the articles he wrote about Sharpton. And so, it was noteworthy that Barrett's postmortem book had virtually nothing on Al Sharpton, short of a casual mention about a detail in 1994, when Mayor Rudy Giuliani "refused to meet with Al Sharpton and others over a police raid at a Harlem mosque."

The absence of Sharpton is surprising to some because the book otherwise contains edited versions of articles Barrett had written about a number of New Yorkers, not just Trump. There was Giuliani, for instance, and a range of others, resurrecting their misdeeds and their flawed characters. Included among them are Ramon Velez (the late sleazy anti-poverty hustler from the South Bronx); and former Manhattan Borough President Andrew Stein, mostly forgotten figures.

Into the twenty-first century, almost all working journalists had made peace with Rev. Al. In the summer of 2020, I asked Sharpton if he could think of any journalist, beyond Barrett, who had continued to so openly and continually question his motives and sincerity: "I don't know anyone but Barrett," he said.

There are some very close to Wayne Barrett who say they personally saw a mellowing in Barrett's feelings about Sharpton. Plus, one could surely imagine Barrett's asking himself in his final years: Why waste energy and ink bashing Sharpton? America's biggest menace to truth-telling, by far, is Donald Trump.

7

⬛⬛⬛

Roots of a Preacher's Strength

WHEN I MENTIONED to people that I was writing about Rev. Al Sharpton, I'd sometimes be asked, "Is he really a minister?" Some of them bluntly declared that he was not in fact a minister. Many whites and elite Blacks just did not see religiosity in the images of past decades. Touring with James Brown didn't lend an aura of religiosity, even though R&B music is steeped in the Black soul. The Rev.'s connections to boxing promoter Don King didn't help. Nor did his touring with Michael Jackson, who raised eyebrows with some for his creepy associations with young boys and his plastic face.

In fact, there are four father figures in Sharpton's early life who stand out, especially, for their ties to the Black church. Those four were all ordained men of the cloth, preachers. They helped to make Black Christianity a foundation of Sharpton's identity and, in the end, helped him survive the slings and arrows that were flung his way over time by investigative agencies, by police, and by journalists. Each of the four father figures made a mark on New York City. Two left indelible marks on the nation. All had lasting impacts on Rev. Al Sharpton.

They were Bishop Frederick Douglas Washington, Rev. William Augustus Jones, Rev. Jesse Jackson, and Rev. Adam Clayton Powell Jr.

In 2000, I wrote a 2,000-word entry on Al Sharpton for the *African American Lives* encyclopedia, published by Oxford University Press in association with Harvard's W. E. B. Du Bois Institute, which has since become the Hutchins Center for African & African American Research. I argued that it was impossible to make sense of Al Sharpton without knowing about his childhood paternal abandonment and the impact that had on Sharpton's mother and Sharpton himself. It was a classic instance of Freudian trauma. It is accepted now by many as a root cause of the violence and early deaths that have haunted Black males, especially in urban centers such as Chicago and New York.

When Sharpton was nine-and-a-half years old, Sharpton's father, Alfred Sr., began a romantic relationship with the girl whom the boy preacher's mother, Ada, had borne before marrying Alfred Sr. That offspring of Ada Sharpton's was named Ernestine, called Tina by her mother and the rest of the Sharpton family. Tina was a teenager at the time. The reality of his father's having sex with—and then moving in with—a girl who was little Al's half-sister was mentally crushing to the boy. It devastated Ada Sharpton, and she had what her son later came to believe was a nervous breakdown. Plus, the abandoned household, which included Rev. Al's slightly older sister Cheryl, had to go on welfare.

Tina and Alfred Sr. had a son, who later in life began using the name Kenneth Sharpton Glasgow. In recent years, Glasgow has eerily assumed a role of minister/activist in the state of Alabama, where he lives. He's spent time in local jails for crimes that were not necessarily civil rights related but, rather, had to do with drugs and violence. Like his half-brother Rev. Al, Rev. Kenneth did not earn a degree in theology. He has been outspoken on the need for prison reform and for the rights of the formerly incarcerated. One senses an invisible nexus between the two male Sharptons. But one can also discern a hesitancy and even a suffused resentment. Rev. Kenneth is, after all, Rev. Al's half-brother—and his nephew. Anyone with a modicum of sensitivity to Freudian trauma would understand conflicts in the relationship.

But back when he was a boy, life went on for little Alfred. Such can be the outcome when one is surrounded by love and care. Ada Sharpton, little Alfred's mom, was a religious woman. Back in the 1950s, before the father deserted the household, Ada Sharpton had taken Alfred and sister Cheryl to experience God and, she hoped, salvation at the Washington Temple Church of God in Christ, located in Central Brooklyn. It was pastored by Bishop Frederick Douglas Washington. (The nineteenth-century Black abolitionist Frederick Douglass used two *ss* in his name. But the Washington Temple consistently uses one *s* for the bishop's middle name.)

The Temple was Pentecostal, as distinguished from Baptist and other mainstream Christian denominations. Little Alfred took a liking to the bishop, the way he spoke, his constant busyness, his ease with his admiring congregants, and the passion and fluidity of his sermons. The lad soon began preaching himself, first at home to his sister Cheryl's dolls. Bishop Washington and others at the church took note of the boy's uncommon talents at the pulpit. At the age of ten, Sharpton received from Washington a certification that established him as a preacher at the congregation. Alfred was thereafter known as the "boy preacher" and as Rev. Alfred. No formal schooling was involved. Nor, actually, was it unusual for Black ministers to achieve their status that way. Some middle-class Black Episcopalians and Methodists sniffed dismissively at that fact. They referred to that path to the ministry as "turning your collar around." Little Rev. Alfred began preaching, sometimes getting paid for his sermons, and even on occasion accompanying the famous gospel singer Mahalia Jackson. He would stand and boom on pulpits at churches over the coming fifty years but would never have a church of his own.

Some Black elites also looked down on Pentecostals for the "whoopin' and hollerin'" that made Sunday services so meaningful to many working-class southern Blacks. Plus, as talented and active as Bishop Washington was in the community, midcentury Pentecostals were generally not as involved in local and national politics as others were, especially the Baptists. (See the works of Clarence Taylor, scholar of Black religion and author of numerous works, especially *The Black Churches of Brooklyn*, published in 1994 by Columbia University Press.)

There came a time, when Alfred was in his teens, that Ada Sharpton felt her son needed to be with a minister whose work and reputation would offer strong chances for a life of meaningful leadership for her son. And so, mom had Alfred introduced to Rev. William Augustus Jones. Jones not only came from a southern, academic-rooted, preaching lineage, but he was one of those Blacks who were associated in the minds of many with the Rev. Martin Luther King Jr. and with anti-racism protests evolving in Black Brooklyn during the 1960s. Rev. Jones was a key figure in early 1960s protests against discrimination in the construction industry in Brooklyn, and in the 1970s he led protests against the huge supermarket chain A&P. He stood out not just for his booming voice at the pulpit but also for his intellectual qualities. In 1979 he published a book titled *God in the Ghetto* (Progressive Baptist Publishing House of Elgin, Illinois), which is erudite and scholarly in its language and source citations. The book offers a back-looking view of the Black church in America, capturing the pains and challenges of Black Christians struggling at grassroots as well as elite levels across the country. It notes the psychological impact of their shared slavery past.

Even as the boy preacher Alfred Sharpton shifted to Rev. Jones, he maintained a respect for and connection with Bishop Washington, who had spiritually birthed him. Rev. Jones, active in national Baptist organizations and political groups, began taking on Sharpton almost as an adopted child. (Rev. Jones had four children of his own, a son and three daughters.) It was Rev. Jones who in 1969 introduced young Sharpton to an early rising star of Black ministry and politics, the Rev. Jesse Jackson.

Jackson, based in Chicago, and Jones, in Brooklyn, were involved in Operation Breadbasket, which had been set up by civil rights leaders to make demands on white businesses for fair treatment of Blacks around the country. One day Jackson came in from Chicago and met with Jones on Fulton Street near Nostrand Avenue in Bedford-Stuyvesant. They were going to have a ribbon-cutting ceremony for the official opening of Operation Breadbasket in Brooklyn. Jones brought Alfred Sharpton with him into the room where Jackson was sitting.

Jones said to Jackson, "Country, this is Alfred Sharpton. He's gonna be our youth leader." "Country" was a name Blacks "up north" often used for Blacks more recently arrived from the South. Significantly, it was also an appellation pinned on Jesse Jackson, who was on a path to legendary status in America. He had been there with Rev. Martin Luther King Jr. at the Lorraine Motel in Memphis when King was assassinated in 1968. Soon after that, the famous musician and composer Cannonball Adderley composed a song titled "Country Preacher" that was a homily to Jesse Jackson. It was recorded at a church in Chicago and it gave praise to the Southern Christian Leadership Conference and its Operation Breadbasket, which was run by Jackson in Chicago and Jones in New York.

Rev. Al, recalling his introduction to Jesse Jackson in Brooklyn, said Jackson looked at him and gave him the first of countless words of advice he'd offer over the coming decades.

"Choose your targets and kick ass," Sharpton said Jackson told him. "Here was this big guy with a big Afro and buckskin vest. . . . I fell in love with Jesse Jackson. . . . He became my model. It was set in my mind. I made that conclusion—I can do this."

Sharpton sensed that he and Jackson had parallel life trajectories. Sharpton says that his three other father figures who were ministers had "high lineage" of which neither Jackson nor Sharpton could boast. Those ministers had ancestors who had also been educated preachers. And, significantly, their fathers spent time at home with them while they were growing up. "All three of these [other] role models that I had had a pedigree and lineage that I didn't have,"

Sharpton said. "[Rev.] Bill Jones was a third-generation big preacher whose father and grandfather had been pastors of big churches, going to the best schools available to Blacks at that time." (Jones, who died in 2006 at the age of seventy-one, had been born in Louisville, Kentucky.) Of Bishop Washington, who was from Arkansas, Sharpton said: "His father had been a bishop, and his grandfather a preacher. He was in the high elite of the Pentecostal Church." And as for Adam Clayton Powell, "His daddy was the biggest preacher in New York, when he was growin' up [in the early decades of the 1900s]. Adam Clayton Powell went to Colgate University. [He] was well refined. I had none of that lineage, none of that pedigree."

Adam Clayton Powell Jr.

Sharpton says his ties to Adam Clayton Powell were more complicated than his links to the other ministers.

Sharpton was in his late teens when he connected with Powell, one of the most controversial and politically influential figures in early twentieth-century Black New York and America.

Powell, who was very fair-complexioned (almost white-looking), was the pastor of the historic Abyssinian Baptist Church in Harlem. Powell was going through especially challenging struggles in the late 1960s. But young Sharpton sensed an inner power that gave the minister/politician strength to make it through those trials, personal and political.

Powell began his rise to public attention in the 1930s. He led angry street demonstrations against hiring discrimination by shopkeepers in Harlem. Powell went on to make history by becoming the first Black elected to the New York City Council. Then, in 1944, he won a seat in the U.S. Congress representing Harlem and became the first Black member of Congress from New York State.

Sharpton had actually first seen Powell in the 1950s when the little boy Sharpton was roaming the halls of Washington Memorial Pentecostal Church. "I went out in the sanctuary and I saw this tall, what seemed to be, white guy smoking a cigar. I said, 'Bishop Washington, there's a white guy coming in.' It was Adam Clayton Powell." Powell had a relationship with Washington and had been using his political influence to help the bishop, as Powell did for many other ministers and community leaders in New York. Sharpton realized he had seen a powerhouse, and so he joined the Youth Committee for Adam Clayton Powell.

Watching Powell on the news and hearing others talk about him in the late 1960s, Sharpton wanted to meet Powell on the minister's home turf, over at the Abyssinian Baptist Church in Harlem. So the teenager got his mom to agree to let big sister Cheryl take him to Abyssinian by subway. The two entered Abyssinian Church and, to the boy's lasting delight, Powell recognized him right away as the "wonder boy preacher" from Bishop Washington's church. In one of Sharpton's autobiographies, *Go and Tell Pharaoh*, Sharpton recalls Powell's saying they should all go to the Red Rooster for a drink. Sharpton declined, pointing out that he was ten years old. (Sharpton said in 2020 interviews that he never drank or used drugs. It was widely known that Powell did drink more liquor than he should have. One perhaps questionable habit Sharpton maybe did pick up from Powell, however, was the smoking of cigars. Sharpton would indulge himself with artfully rolled tobacco into the twenty-first century, as he became a big shot schmoozing with media personalities, actors, and others in swanky Manhattan locales.)

Sharpton cherished his time with Powell back in the '60s. He learned what it was like to suffer pressures that were aired in the newspapers and on television. He learned how meaningful it was to manifest courage and boldness in spite of all the tribulations.

In 1967, a U.S. House of Representatives Select Committee found that Powell had committed acts of financial misconduct, using public funds for personal use. There had also been other embarrassing activities that possibly were related to his heavy drinking. He fought legal battles with the Congress over his claims that he should be allowed to continue representing his Harlem district. In a strange (and literal) move, in 1970 he began spending most of his time in the Bahamas and resigned as the pastor of Harlem's Abyssinian Baptist Church. Later that year, in June 1970, he lost the Democratic primary to the challenger for his seat in the Congress. That was Charles Rangel, who would win the general election and remain as Harlem's congressman for forty-six years.

Of the four preacher father figures, Sharpton says, Powell was not among the top three in terms of the hours he spent with them; but Powell mattered in the lessons he taught about struggling in life, against inner and outer foes.

Seeing the Heights

In Rev. Jesse Jackson, young Sharpton could see that it was possible to rise from the bottom to the top. He wanted to be like him.

"Jesse was born out of wedlock, came out of a dysfunctional home like I did. His mother had to make it the best way she could. Jesse dropped out of seminary, Chicago [Theological] seminary, like I dropped out of Brooklyn College. He was the youngest one on [Martin Luther] King's staff, and he wore a dashiki."

Dashikis were the African garment that had become stylish among Black college students and Black nationalists in the 1960s. Sharpton would begin wearing a dashiki in the late '60s. And he shaped his hair into a bushy Afro, like the one Jesse Jackson sported.

Jesse Jackson in the 1980s would go on to firmly establish himself in U.S. politics by making serious Democratic primary runs for the presidency. In doing so he heightened Black enthusiasm for the electoral process around the country, very notably in New York State. It must be pointed out that during the years of Tawana Brawley tensions, 1988 and '89, Jackson was vigilant and cautious about over-identifying with Sharpton.

By the beginning of the twenty-first century, informed commentators would note tensions, and embedded rivalries, between Jackson and Sharpton. (In 2004 Sharpton himself made a run for the Democratic nomination for president.)

Pentecostal to Baptist (with Tawana in Between)

A key to understanding the political significance of Black Christianity in the Brooklyn of Sharpton's youth is this: Large numbers of working-class Blacks from the South were Pentecostals, a designation that takes in those who worshiped at churches with "Church of God in Christ" in their names. Early on, which is to say in the 1930s through early '60s, the Pentecostals often stayed remote from politics. They dissociated themselves from the Black clubhouses where an emerging educated Black middle class was gathering to seek judgeships, high-end jobs in education, and other positions in civil service.

The distancing had understandable history to it. Black Christian worship in the slavery-era South hid cruel realities beneath allegories of a world-to-come, when freedom and justice would reign. To have prayed aloud for that life of freedom to be here and now would have drawn violent reaction. Black religion scholar Clarence Taylor says that religious singing during slavery had Old Testament references, and the new post-slavery era hymns were based openly on the New Testament, with Jesus Christ as the symbol of coming salvation and ultimate victory. That latter poetic suffusion lived in the minds and voices of many Pentecostal Blacks through the mid–twentieth century. (See Taylor's chapter on "Holiness–Pentecostal Culture" in his book *Black Churches of Brooklyn*. He cites, along with copious other pieces of evidence, a 1900 composition of the long-deceased Charles Price Jones, "I'm Happy with Jesus Alone.")

For the most part, it was Baptist pastors in mid-twentieth-century Brooklyn who had the greatest impact in local politics, by reason of their education at theological colleges and their comfort in exchanges with Black and white powerbrokers.

Thus, many up-and-coming Black elites in Brooklyn were strongly attracted, in the 1960s and beyond, to Rev. William August Jones of Bethany Baptist Church.

(Interestingly, Clarence Taylor points out that in the mid–twentieth century Black Baptist ministers tended to be Republicans. This would be notable in political leanings also of Pentecostal ministers who would become involved in local politics. In 2020, I asked Rev. Al about his decision in 1986 to back the conservative Republican candidate for a U.S. Senate seat representing New York, Alfonse D'Amato, considered by many to be racist in some of his public comments. There had been reports that Sharpton had supported D'Amato because he'd cut a deal with him, expecting D'Amato to use influence to obtain funding for Sharpton's National Youth Movement. No money ever changed hands, reports have shown. In any event, Sharpton told me he backed D'Amato in that race because D'Amato was the choice of Sharpton's pastor at the Washington Temple, Bishop Frederick D. Washington.)

But it's noteworthy and relevant that Rev. William Augustus Jones, the Bethany Baptist Church pastor who introduced Sharpton to Jesse Jackson, was left-leaning and aligned with Democrats. Jones stayed fairly close to Sharpton throughout the 1970s and even into the late 1980s when Sharpton was in his most controversial period. But there would come a time, in the early '90s, when he admitted to having had concerns about Sharpton's actions and political decisions in the 1970s and '80s.

In 1988, Rev. Jones opened up his Bethany church to Sharpton and the Tawana Brawley family. The New York Attorney General was trying to get them to testify about Tawana's alleged rape. Prosecutors threatened to arrest Glenda, the mother, if she continued to refuse to cooperate, but they made it clear they would not force their way into a church in order to reach her. Sharpton didn't want either of the Brawleys compelled to give testimony. So he reached out to Jones and asked that the Brawleys be given "shelter" at Bethany. The minister/father-figure agreed.

Bill Randolph, a longtime trustee of Bethany Baptist Church, recalled those weeks when Glenda and Tawana Brawley were sequestered at the church in 1988. Speaking with me in 2020, he said some members of the church disagreed with the decision to shelter the Brawleys, but they held their pastor in high regard and went along with his decision.

At Bethany, reporters covering the Brawley story showed up to press conferences put together by Sharpton and the two Brawley attorneys. One occasion stood out strongly for the city's reporters. Some journalists saw the incident as both revealing and comical. He did not come out and say so, but it must have been an embarrassment for the pastor, Rev. Jones.

It was Saturday, June 11, 1988. Reporters and photographers from around New York went to the church hoping to get quotes and photos from Sharpton, Maddox, and Mason. Even as they began entering the church, journalists were greeted with hostile glances and verbal insults. Perhaps a dozen news outlets had shown up. About 200 loud supporters of Tawana Brawley and Sharpton were there. Some Black reporters felt a special discomfort. The Brawley team had long been criticizing some Black journalists as "lackeys" of the white media, as sell-outs who didn't know what it meant to be truly Black. Speaking with me in April 2021, former *Newsday* reporter Clem Richardson, who is Black, recalled that day at Bethany. He was there with two other *Newsday* reporters, both also Black.

"They just started railing against the press, *Newsday* particularly," Richardson said, referring to Sharpton and his backers.

(The resentment of *Newsday* had to do largely with *Newsday*'s articles from earlier that year, when the paper revealed Sharpton's past work with the FBI. In addition, some rally organizers had suspicions about Les Payne, the Black *Newsday* columnist who later exposed the Brawley rape story as made up.)

"Everyone from *Newsday* stand up," attorney Mason bellowed. Richardson stood and then another Black reporter, Michael Cottman, did also. Mason shouted that three *Newsday* reporters were known to be in the church and they all had to stand up.

That third "reporter" was a recently hired twenty-year-old intern, Juliette Fairley, Black and from San Antonio, Texas. Recently arrived in New York, she was sitting next to Richardson and appeared all but frozen by what she was experiencing.

Speaking to me in 2021, Richardson said, "Some guy tried to reach around me and tried to make her stand up." He was referring to one of the Brawley team's security people, who actually put his hands on the intern. "I'm standing. She doesn't have to," said Richardson, who is six feet, five inches tall.

"Everybody started chanting and screaming, and there was this whole brouhaha," Richardson said. "We were ushered out the side door."

To the disappointment of Sharpton and the Brawley attorneys, reporters from other news organizations walked out in solidarity with the *Newsday* crew. Among the other news outlets were the *Daily News*, the *New York Times*, the *Poughkeepsie Journal*, the *Associated Press*, and *United Press International*. According to *Newsday*'s June 12 article, a Brawley team representative, Curtis Stewart, went outside and told journalists that only *Newsday* reporters had been ordered to leave and that all the others should go back in. They declined. (A Black *Daily News* reporter, Lyle Harris, said he left the rally out of solidarity, saying he believed they had been trying to cover the Brawley story with honesty and faithfulness to the principles of journalism. He was quoted in the *Newsday* story of June 12, 1988.)

Fairley, the intern, was shocked by what she went through that day. "To me it was devastating," she told me, speaking by phone in April 2021. Fairley went on to earn a master's from the Columbia University Graduate School of Journalism and began working as a freelance writer and actor in New York City.

Reflecting on her experience at Bethany, Fairley she told me it revealed embedded truths about New York City, Al Sharpton, and Black religion.

"I was so young, just off the boat from Texas, my first time in New York," she said. "I really didn't know how racial politics worked in New York. I came from the South where Blacks tended to be together more" when it came to controversial local issues.

Regarding intra-group tensions in the Black community, the Tawana Brawley story was meaningful and painful for Fairley. Sharpton used to go around saying that Blacks believed the Tawana Brawley rape story because white men historically had gotten away with raping Black women. Sharpton once looked around a room and told the listeners that the light-complexioned ones among them were proof of those past rapes. Fairley told me there were some at Bethany who made disparaging remarks about her complexion. Fairley was the proud daughter of a white mother and a Black father.

She didn't have precise phrases that were used, but she said it was obvious to her that "I was being singled out because I was light-skinned."

Pertinent to the topic of white-on-Black rape, Fairley told me she had a great-great-grandmother, Georgianna Dudley, who in 1893 was raped by a white man in Brownsville, South Carolina. Her great-grandmother Mary Dudley was a product of that rape. "Oh, no," she answered when I asked if the white man had been identified and formally accused. "White men were not prosecuted for that."

But the experience of her great-great-grandmother and Tawana Brawley had nothing in common, she said.

Interestingly, Fairley said that two years before, in 2019, she went as a freelancer to cover a Manhattan press conference held by New

York City Comptroller Scott Stringer. She was surprised to see Al Sharpton there.

"I think he recognized me," she said. "He looked at me for a long time. I held his gaze. But I didn't say anything. What am I going to say to the man?" (Asked by me to comment, Sharpton said by phone in April 2021 that he did not remember Fairley at all, from Stringer's press conference or from Bethany in 1988. He also said he did not recall the incident of *Newsday* reporters' being kicked out of Bethany.)

Fairley sees old-fashioned journalists as would-be truth-tellers. Black ministers are truth-tellers, she acknowledged. But sometimes the impulse to be wealthy or powerful interferes with the high calling, she said.

"A reverend who was not looking for national attention probably would not have" behaved as Sharpton did at Bethany Church that day in 1988, Fairley said. Sharpton and Jesse Jackson "kind of took that model that Martin Luther King created and took it to a whole new level."

But Sharpton deserves credit for using his natural gifts to soar to the heights of earthly achievement, Fairley said. "He just was doing his thing, climbing up the ladder. He was so theatrical. I was just part of the show," she said, referring to the events of June 11, 1988.

"That's what his gifts are and he used [them] to get to the top. He's doing better than everybody.

"The rest of us journalists, we're writers. For me, 'making it' means I have a roof over my head and I have food on the table, and I haven't sold my soul."

Rev. Jones, one of Sharpton's father figures and the pastor of Bethany Baptist Church, clearly began entertaining second thoughts about the propriety of some of Sharpton's actions.

Rev. Jones opened up about his relationship with Sharpton in a 1993 article written by reporter Jim Sleeper. The article was "Man of Too Many Parts," a 10,000-word profile that was published in *The New Yorker* magazine. Among many others, Sleeper interviewed Rev. Jones, who expressed a wish that Sharpton had restrained himself in some of the controversial actions he'd taken in the past.

Jones said he knew Sharpton as "a young man with rare endowments who got pulled into many conflicting directions." He also revealed a specific personal disappointment, saying he would have preferred Sharpton to have taken an established path to acquiring his religious collar. "I really wanted him to go to a college, then to seminary, to become fully credentialed."

Though Sharpton never returned to college, as Jones had wanted, the boy turned man did something else that showed his fondness for Rev. Jones. He became a Baptist, shedding the Pentecostal identity that had been with him since childhood.

In a well-attended ceremony, Rev. Jones baptized Sharpton at Bethany Baptist Church in July 1994. "[T]he progressive Baptist church is the tradition of Rev. Martin Luther King Jr. and Rev. Jesse Jackson," Sharpton said afterward. (Sharpton was quoted in a *New York Times* article, written by Charisse Jones and published July 7, 1994.) Along with his wife, Kathy, and daughters, Dominique and Ashley, Rev. Jackson was present for the baptism.

Bethany Baptist first opened its doors to the Black faithful in 1883. In 1924, it became the first Black church to move into the area then called the Bedford section, which would later, in the 1940s, be known as Bedford-Stuyvesant. It was there on Marcus Garvey Boulevard that the Brawleys stayed in 1988.

Tom Wolfe and the "New Journalism"

What we are here calling the Golden Age of journalism, existing very roughly during the second half of the twentieth century, was marked by chapters that defined journalism as a craft. High on the list was the 1970s Watergate saga and the way two young scribes went about doing their stories and helping to bring down a president, Richard Nixon. Those two were Bob Woodward and Carl Bernstein. Rising just behind the Watergate stars was a new generation of journalists inspired by the investigative skills of the Watergate duo. This new cohort tended to be well educated and often alumni of elite universities and graduate schools of journalism. High on the list of desired accomplishments for many was to be taken seriously as a writer.

Les Payne, the Black *Newsday* editor/columnist who had exposed the Tawana Brawley rape allegation as false, once came to speak to a journalism class of mine at Brooklyn College. I remember him saying, "When I started out, like so many journalists back then, what I wanted to do more than anything else was write the Great American Novel." He did not go on to write novels, but he often wrote stories that read like novels, and he went on to write the celebrated biography of Malcolm X, *The Dead Are Arising*. Les Payne admired those who practiced what came to be called the New Journalism.

That term has been interpreted to mean those who could write nonfiction in a gripping style, getting the reader to take in every paragraph as if they were reading suspense stories. Some of the New Journalism writers became household names. There was Truman Capote who wrote the 1966 "true crime novel" *In Cold Blood*, which sold millions of copies and was published in thirty languages. Some journalists, like Jimmy Breslin and Pete Hamill, wrote novels on the side as they did columns for their newspapers.

They were becoming new kings and queens of the two-centuries-old craft of American journalism. Al Sharpton was dealing with this new cohort of fast-fingered journalists.

Perhaps the one who, in the waning years of the twentieth century, earned the most kudos in this New Journalism form was Tom Wolfe.

Like Sharpton, Wolfe had roots in the American South, Sharpton's parents from Alabama and Florida, Wolfe having been born and raised in Virginia. Unlike Sharpton, he was white and grew up privileged, having had a father who was the editor of *The Southern Planter*, an agriculture magazine in Richmond. A natural writer and achiever, Wolfe earned a doctorate in American Studies at Yale University. Wolfe would stroll about town clad in the tailored suits of an old Southern white aristocrat: white jacket, white pants, and white hat. His high life and conservative leanings led some to dismiss him with the moniker Honoré de Redneck.

But in the 1970s Wolfe commanded great respect among white journalists and elite readers in New York City and across the nation. He had been a reporter at a number of newspapers, including the *Washington Post*, before becoming a literary star. He came to be especially known for an article about wealthy New York City leftists. Published in *New York* magazine on June 8, 1970, the story and its headline lived a long life. It was "Radical Chic: That Party at Lenny's." It was about Leonard Bernstein, the famous composer, conductor, and pianist.

Earlier that year, in January, Bernstein had hosted a fundraiser in the living room of his high-end Manhattan dwelling for leaders of the Black Panther Party. Guests contributed thousands of dollars and engaged in discussions with Panther Party members, including Donald Cox, the Panther field marshal and a member of the party's central committee.

Conservatives were furious with Bernstein. And no one in the universe of journalism caused more agony for Bernstein than Tom Wolfe. His scathing, 25,000-word critique was eventually published as part of a book, *Radical Chic & the Mau-Mauing of the Flak*

Catchers. That second part of the title described what Wolfe portrayed as the welfare culture of Blacks, as seen through an anti-poverty program in San Francisco. Wolfe used the term "mau-mauing" to label the perceived tendency of Black militants to shout and make threats of violence in order to obtain money, be it from white businesses or the government.

In 1987, Wolfe came out with a novel that was a celebrated page-turner of its time. Many praised it as speaking relevantly about the social/political transformations befalling New York City at that moment. Not only did it endure at the top of best seller lists, but it also became a must-see movie, produced by Brian De Palma and starring Tom Hanks, Bruce Willis, and Melanie Griffith. It was *The Bonfire of the Vanities*.

One of the central characters was a loud Black minister who billed himself as a seeker of justice for Blacks in New York City but who showed questionable motives. The name of the street-shouting preacher was Rev. Reginald Bacon. The writer struck me as having deep-rooted notions of Black ministers as jack-legs, whoopin' and hollerin', and jive timin' every white person they come across. I asked myself, at the first sight of the name Rev. Bacon, "Why Rev. Bacon? Why not go all the way and call him Rev. Porkchop? or Watermelon?" The book to me was like a novelistic revival of Wolfe's 1970s book about Black anti-poverty pimps "mau-mauing" their way to livelihoods.

In January 1991, a reporter for *Entertainment Weekly* interviewed Al Sharpton at the opening of the movie *Bonfire of the Vanities*. Those familiar with the book and movie saw Sharpton under the name Rev. Bacon. The reporter, Meredith Berkman, was eyeing Sharpton during the showing. Sharpton's reaction, when pressed by *EW* for comment, was consistent with that of an activist whose Black American roots remained at his core:

"This is insulting," he said. "So far, there's not a civilized black in the whole movie. They're thieves, crooks, gangsters. David Duke should have directed this movie," he added, referring to the Louisiana Ku Klux Klan leader. ("Al Sharpton on 'Bonfire of the Vanities,'" *Entertainment Weekly*, January 18, 1991.)

Speaking with me in 2020, Sharpton said, with a bit of anger still beneath his voice, "The media should have challenged" Wolfe about the racism in *Bonfire of the Vanities*.

The media were derelict.

(What I didn't know back then, but came to learn in doing research for this book, was that the founding pastor of Sharpton's beloved Bethany Baptist Church, back in 1883, was a Rev. Joseph Bacon, the same surname as Tom Wolfe's stand-in for Sharpton. Whether Wolfe knew that, I can't say. But it would make sense that a New Journalism star with strong investigative skills would, indeed, have known. Wolfe died in 2018.)

Becoming an Acknowledged Thought Leader

In his book *Black Religious Intellectuals: The Fight for Equality from Jim Crow to the 21st Century*, Clarence Taylor, the Baruch College scholar of Black theology, gives Sharpton one of the most credible and authoritative nods of approval Sharpton had received until then. Taylor made it clear that he was examining Sharpton at a transitional moment. The book was published in 2002.

Taylor noted that the newspapers which had once seemed poised to remove him from the public stage had lately been affirming the seriousness of Sharpton's actions. He writes about the Rev. as an emerging thought-leader. The title of the chapter devoted to Sharpton is "A Natural Born Leader." It appears to foresee the impact that the still-rising Sharpton would come to have on New York City and America further into the new century.

8

"I Know Jews from Italians"

IN JIM SLEEPER'S 1993 *New Yorker* profile of Sharpton, "A Man of Too Many Parts," Sharpton told the writer that he was different from the controversial attorney Alton Maddox, who had advised the Tawana Brawley family. Maddox was raised in Georgia, and Sharpton in Brooklyn, he advised. Therefore, "I know Jews from Italians."

Al Sharpton's ability to deal with white reporters, Catholic or Jewish, was impressive. This was shown in the way he made peace with and continued friendly contact with Mike McAlary, the *New York Newsday* reporter on the team that broke the story about Sharpton's work with the FBI. The Irish were the old-timers in New York City, having diminished as a demographic core by the mid–twentieth century. The Irish continued to stand out in the newspaper world and in the upper echelons of the New York City Police Department, but the new white demographic surging in post–World War II New York City would consist of Italians and Jews.

As Sharpton was coming of age, the 1950s through the '80s, a hugely growing population of Blacks in Brooklyn began dealing with the Jews and Italians. Both of those white ethnic groups had together become the major economic and political forces running the borough.

The relations between Black Brooklynites and Italians were often conflicted in ways that were more likely to be physical than was the case with Jews. The attacks on Blacks that led to big news stories in the 1980s occurred in Italian American neighborhoods. Young Blacks in the 1960s and '70s often felt those areas were not safe for them to be strolling through.

Sharpton, however, says he recalls gentle relationships with Italians from his childhood. In his autobiographies, for instance, he writes of his father's closeness to (and business dealings with) Italians who owned buildings in eastern Brooklyn—that is, Brownsville and East New York.

Sharpton says further that, as he grew up, he came to know Italian Americans connected with the entertainment business, and from there he says he learned that the Italian mob had a strong hold over the music industry, notably the sector with Black artists. Speaking with me in 2020, Sharpton said he planned to write a book on the mob and the Black music industry of that era. (Sharpton's connections with mob figures have been referred to previously in this book and are contained especially in the writings of mob reporter William Bastone.)

But while Sharpton linked Italians with Jews in describing his Brooklyn upbringing, it was the Jewish community that stood out for expressing feelings of hostility toward Sharpton.

The Label That Lasted Decades—Anti-Semite

American Jews had established a reputation for being sympathetic to demands being made by Blacks in the civil rights era. They stood out among white ethnics for involvement in sit-ins and marches to end racial segregation in the South during the 1950s and '60s.

But in New York City of the 1970s, notably in Brooklyn, frictions surfaced between Blacks and Jews. The neighborhood that stood out for exhibiting those tensions was Crown Heights. Migration from the South and immigration from the Caribbean led to a surge in the numbers of Blacks in and around Crown Heights. Added to that was the fact that the Jews who had begun settling there, midcentury, were Lubavitch Hasidim. The Hasidic Jews were nowhere near as liberal-minded as the secular Jews who, for example, went to demonstrate for Black rights in the South, nor were they as socially open as many of the working-class Jews of New York City, who worked in civil service jobs with Blacks and developed friendships with them. The Hasidim were insular and self-protective. For example, private Hasidic patrols in the 1970s began targeting Black men, following them through the neighborhood and making reports to police or sometimes approaching the men to question them. Such encounters were foundational to the community tensions that erupted in the bloody Crown Heights disturbances of 1991.

(Note to the reader: I wrote the above based on readings but also on having spent my childhood and young adulthood in Central Brooklyn, which includes Crown Heights.)

The Crown Heights disturbances began on August 19, 1991. A caravan of cars was transporting Hasidic Rabbi Menachem Mendel Schneerson, leader of the Chabad Lubavitch Hasidic movement, along Utica Avenue in Crown Heights. The vehicles were led by a New York City Police Department escort and had the right to go through red lights. But one of the cars crashed into a stone pillar and killed a seven-year-old boy, Gavin Cato, son of immigrants from Guyana. When a Hasidic ambulance arrived, witnesses said its responders ignored Gavin and directed their attention to the injured Hasidic Jews. Blacks flared up in anger. There were counter-reactions from local Jews.

Several hours after rioting began, around midnight, a twenty-nine-year-old Orthodox Jewish student from Australia, Yankel Rosenbaum, was fatally beaten and stabbed. Before his death at nearby Kings County Hospital, he identified a Black teenager, Lemrick Nelson, as the main attacker among many. (Some were reported to have been shouting "Kill the Jew!")

Nelson was acquitted in the initial murder trial but was hit with other charges, including violating Rosenbaum's civil rights, and he served ten years in prison. Jews in New York maintained that the Blacks on the original jury did not vote to convict out of a shared anti-Semitism, and anger has remained to the present day.

Jewish groups said Sharpton stirred up tensions. In 2001, the brother of the murdered Yankel Rosenbaum, Norman Rosenbaum, reflected on Sharpton in a *New York Daily News* column, recalling the riots of ten years before. Norman Rosenbaum wrote of comments said to have been uttered by Sharpton and quoted in a number of Jewish newspapers. "Talk about how Oppenheimer in South Africa sends diamonds straight to Tel Aviv and deals with the diamond merchants right here in Crown Heights. The issue is not anti-Semitism; the issue is apartheid. . . . All we want to say is what Jesus said: 'If you offend one of these little ones, you got to pay for it' . . . ." (Sharpton's quote appeared somewhat differently in various outlets, but the essential phrases were consistent.)

Sharpton offended Jews on other occasions. For instance, in 1988, when Sharpton was refusing New York State Attorney General Robert Abrams's demand to meet with Sharpton about Tawana Brawley, Sharpton was widely quoted as saying that meeting with Abrams would be "like asking someone who watched someone killed in the gas chamber to sit down with Mr. Hitler." Abrams is Jewish.

On the topic of Black anti-Semitism, the public figure who stood out most for being guilty of that in those days was Louis Farrakhan. Farrakhan had taken over the leadership of the old Nation of Islam (from which Malcolm X had sprung and had parted ways). Farrakhan's remarks over the decades had been crude, Hitlerian, and embarrassing to any Black person with Jewish friends or a sense of decency.

And, yes, it's true that Sharpton partnered frequently with Farrakhan. That happened because Sharpton would partner with anybody who gave him cachet when he needed it. Regarding Farrakhan's cachet, the evidence of it was legion: his podium eloquence; his organization's denunciation of Black criminality that affected Black communities; and, most of all, his inner rapport with the hundreds of thousands of young Black men who convened with him on the National Mall of Washington, D.C., in 1995 for the historic "Million Man March." They came from all economic classes. They were laborers, professionals and college students. They were fed up with Black men's being targets of racist white police officers and fed up with the animus they experienced otherwise in their lives.

As for me, the thing that bothers me about the white Farrakhan haters is this: They ignore what should be the infamy of his involvement in the assassination of Malcolm X. Farrakhan had made threatening public declarations about Malcolm X in the months leading up to the assassination. (By the way, Farrakhan in 1985 told a crowd at Madison Square Garden that David Dinkins should be killed for having criticized Black leaders like Farrakhan.)

Regarding Malcolm X, Farrakhan was not with the assassins at the Audubon Ballroom in Harlem. But Sharpton's Tawana Brawley nemesis, the late journalist Les Payne, mentions in his Malcolm X biography that Farrakhan met secretly in Newark, New Jersey, with anti-Malcolm Nation of Islam leaders right after the assassination. Payne refers to Farrakhan's presence as "possibly incriminating." But that means nothing to those concerned only about anti-Semite labels when it comes to Black leaders.

Sharpton's 2020 march on Washington, conducted during the Covid-19 shutdown, made pre-millennial Black Americans reflect on Farrakhan's larger Million Man March of 1995. Sharpton's event was a reflection both of who he was and who he had become. Any inkling of anti-Semitism had faded away.

Confronted about anti-Semitic statements from the 1990s, Sharpton has always apologized for failing to show the Christian sensitivity he says he now holds dear.

Black/Jewish Tension in Journalism

As for whether anti-Black bias could be found in the writings of some journalists of the old era, the Black scholar Clarence Taylor says yes. And in *Black Religious Intellectuals*, Taylor singles out Jim Sleeper, an identifying Jew, who wrote the expansive 1993 *New Yorker* profile of Al Sharpton. Sleeper would argue, in his writings, that Blacks needed to learn to take the same paths to success that ethnic whites, notably Italians and Jews, had taken.

Sleeper wrote regularly for *The Village Voice, New York Newsday,* and the *New York Daily News.* He also did articles in other influential news outlets. Though Sleeper is Jewish, he wrote often about Blacks and he revealed a long-lasting interest in Al Sharpton.

Taylor suggested there was micro-racism at the core of Sleeper's feelings about Sharpton. He wrote that Sleeper had been "[p]reparing the groundwork for the right-wing ideologue Dinesh D'Souza, who claims in *The End of Racism* that blacks suffer from a civilization gap. . . ." Taylor went on to assert that Sleeper, notably in his book writing, "reconstructs the image of white neighborhoods as romantic utopian communities that suppress difference for the good of the whole." Sleeper is the author of *Liberal Racism: How Fixating on Race Subverts the American Dream,* published by Viking in 1997, and *The Closest of Strangers: Liberalism and the Politics of Race in New York,* published by W. W. Norton & Company in 1991.

"These assertions [of Sleeper's] . . . do little more than construct a simplistic image of the minister from Brooklyn," Taylor wrote in *Black Religious Intellectuals.* "They completely ignore his use of cultural symbolism, his reinterpretation of race and politics, and his efforts to transform himself."

(Personal note from the author: I have loved Jim Sleeper. We overlapped as *Newsday* reporters during the early 1990s. We've also identified as fellow Yale graduates, he in 1969, I in 1970. But I do find it infuriating that Sleeper maintained that Blacks had shortcomings they would not acknowledge—and yet effectively had Black America as a beat, writing about Blacks for the nation's most highly regarded magazines, newspapers, and book publishers. I think that, below the surface, even when we worked together, I winced at this. It was because of this feeling that I declined to be interviewed by him on the record about three decades ago, when he wanted to talk to me about my grandfather Bertram Baker and Baker's experiences in early twentieth-century politics in Brooklyn. (Baker was the subject of my Fordham University Press book *Boss of Black Brooklyn: The Life and Times of Bertram L. Baker.*)

Still, I'm compelled to give credit where it's due. Sleeper's profile of Al Sharpton in *The New Yorker* in 1993 was one of the most thorough pieces written about Sharpton during his pre-twenty-first-century years. I felt that Sleeper mostly covered up his biases in reporting and writing that article. I believe it was a classic example of the truth-seeking and truth-telling that the best journalism colleges in the late twentieth century trained their students to practice.

In the summer of 2020, when Sleeper and I reconnected by phone and e-mail, he had just retired after two decades as a Yale lecturer teaching journalism.

9

The '90s: Climbing the Ladder in Politics

A WARRIOR'S SPIRIT revealed itself in the way Sharpton handled his stabbing on January 12, 1991. As the ambulance was taking him from the site of the stabbing in the Bensonhurst section of Brooklyn to Coney Island Hospital, Rev. Al thought he might very well die. "There were times that I was fearful and there was times that I didn't know what was going to happen," he said, reflecting in 2020. "And I think those are the times that I sit back and introspectively say those were the tests to see if I was really sincere. And I remember laying in that hospital the night they brought me in . . . . I laid in that bed and I didn't know what they were gonna come up with, whether they had to cut into an artery. I didn't know nothing."

After the successful surgery and during the recovery, he recalled, "I thought about it. I said, 'If they say you're gonna be alright, [I'd ask myself] are you gonna keep marchin' or are you going to just walk away from this? 'Cause you could go back and work with Don King. Don King wanted me to do entertainment for him. He was the biggest boxing figure in the world. I could go make a lot of money in that and forget all of this because you could almost get killed. And I laid in that bed . . . and made up my mind, no, that this is what I'm gonna do [protesting and becoming a public figure]. If I live, I'm gonna do this and if I'm permanently damaged, I'm still gonna do this. And that fear and anxiety is what you've gotta overcome to know that this is really what you believe in . . . . And I kept going."

Just several days after being admitted for care, Sharpton was released. And four days after that, he participated in a march across the Brooklyn Bridge, celebrating Martin Luther King Day. With Sharpton crossing the bridge that Monday, January 21, were hundreds of loyal followers, everyday Black and progressive New Yorkers and a couple of politicians/buddies who grew closer and closer to him over the following two decades.

"The doctor [had told me] . . . if you go, at least ride in a wheelchair because you're still not that stable. And I never forget. It was bitter cold because it's January, and I get in a wheelchair and they're wheeling me across the Brooklyn Bridge, three or four hundred people behind me; and I look up to see who's wheeling me and it was State Senator David Paterson [who is legally blind]. And I said, 'For real I'm in trouble now.' I said, 'You get a guy that can't see to be the one to wheel me across the Brooklyn Bridge?' And David Paterson laughed all the way across the bridge."

Sharpton said he formed a special bond with Paterson, whose father, Basil Paterson, was a well-known Harlem politician, and also with Gregory Meeks of Queens, who had ambitions to hold elective office. "We were all around the same age, and so we used to get together and talk about our lives."

A year after Sharpton's stabbing and the march across the Brooklyn Bridge, in 1992, Meeks ran for election to become state assemblyman representing his district in southeast Queens. He ran on the same Democratic primary ticket as Sharpton, who was taking a sky-high shot at becoming a U.S senator from New York. Meeks won his primary contest and then won the general election, fulfilling the dream he'd shared with his buddies Paterson and Sharpton, of becoming an elected official and climbing the ladder from there. (Sharpton came in third out of four in the Democratic primary for the U.S. Senate seat. It was a clear loss, but his respectable showing stunned and impressed state politicians and pundits.) As for Paterson, the state senator in the trio with Sharpton and Meeks, "You know he comes from these eons of political big shots, a family of high regard, and he wanted to be the second Black mayor of New York. He wanted to be our generation's Dave Dinkins."

In 1994, Sharpton made another run to be the Democratic nominee for a U.S. Senate seat representing New York. He lost again, but again he won further credibility regarding his influence with Black voters, especially in New York City. And despite what Sharpton described as Paterson's ambition to be mayor, it was Sharpton who made a high-profile run to be the Democratic nominee against incumbent New York City Mayor Rudolph Giuliani in 1997. Sharpton lost that attempt to former Manhattan Borough President Ruth Messinger, who herself lost the general election to Giuliani. (Paterson stayed on as Harlem's state senator, soon rising to become Minority Leader of the Senate, the New York State Lieutenant Governor, and, in 2008, governor, after Eliot Spitzer had to step down following reports of relationships with prostitutes.)

Sharpton enjoyed recalling a twenty-first-century get-together with David Paterson and Gregory Meeks. It was 2001. This time the buddy meet-up was in Puerto Rico. And Sharpton was in jail.

In May of that year, Sharpton had been in the thick of protests in Puerto Rico against the U.S. Navy's use of the island of Vieques as a bombing site for military exercises. Residents of Vieques felt that their lives were being endangered by the long-running exercises. Sharpton's involvement earned him praises and lasting gratitude from Latinos and union progressives in New York and around the United States. (*Newsday*'s Sheryl McCarthy wryly wrote in a June 10, 2001, syndicated column that his first 16 days in jail in Vieques had earned Sharpton 6,487 stories in New York City newspapers. She conceded the number was her "unofficial estimate.")

Sharpton was arrested on May 1, and on May 23 a federal judge in Puerto Rico sentenced him to a harsh ninety-day sentence for his involvement in the protests.

"[W]hen I was in jail in Vieques, David came and Greg Meeks came . . . . So here I am now in jail, Paterson says, 'Well,' he said, 'looks like a lot of our dreams come true.' I said, 'Well, what do you mean?' He said, 'Well, I'm on my way statewide. I think I'm gonna run for Lieutenant Governor and may be governor one day,' which he did become. 'I'm gonna be the new David Dinkins like we dreamed. And Greg is in Congress . . . And look at you, you're in an orange jumpsuit for civil rights. You're the new Jesse Jackson. We all made it.' And we started laughing . . . ." (Paterson served as New York State's governor for almost three years, until the end of 2010, when Andrew Cuomo was elected governor. Paterson remained active in politics, serving for a time as chairman of the New York State Democratic Party.)

On the National Stage

Sharpton's high point, with regard to national press attention—and political ladder-climbing—was his entrance into the 2004 Democratic presidential primary. Sharpton was one of half a dozen Democrats vying for the chance to face off against President George W. Bush, who was running for a second term.

Sharpton earned praise in news columns and from political strategists for his performances in debates. CNN called him "colorful." But it was clear to just about everyone, from the very beginning, that the Rev. didn't stand a chance of winning. Finally he pulled out, and he gave a speech supporting John Kerry at the National Democratic Convention, on July 27, 2004, in Boston. That day he literally put himself on the national stage and showed off his natural speaking talents to the nation.

The speech was supposed to be eight minutes, max. Sharpton told me that he had met with Democratic Chairman Terry McAuliffe and was given an outline. "We wrote out a speech . . . and we did the sound check," Sharpton recalled. Sharpton went back to his hotel room to make calls. Evening came. He went back to the convention center and saw McAuliffe.

"I said, 'You know . . . I'm not giving that speech,'" Sharpton recalled. "I said if you think I came all this distance to get up here and give a sanitized speech you're wrong.

"As I was walking up the steps, I was structuring it in my mind. People were clapping . . . I'm a preacher, I'm from Bed-Stuy. Extemporaneous is my style. I knew my message . . . So my eight minutes went to twenty-three minutes, because of the applause from the audience. And I'm a preacher and I just got caught up with the audience . . . I've never preached from a manuscript in my life and I certainly didn't do it on the campaign trail. I knew what I wanted to do and that's what I did."

Sharpton shouted from the stage, "We never got the forty acres! We didn't get the mule! So, we decided we would ride this donkey as far as it would take us!" That reference to the braying symbol of the Democratic Party drew thunderous applause.

Sharpton told the attending Democrats (and press), "As I ran for president, I hoped that one child could come out of the ghetto like I did. Could look at me, walk[ing] across the stage, with governors and senators, and know they didn't have to be a drug dealer, they didn't have to be a hoodlum, they didn't have to be a gangster. They could stand up from a broken home, on welfare, and they could run for president of the United States."

All through the twenty-three minutes, the clapping continued, with groups of attendees—Blacks, whites, browns—jumping up when sitting and cheering wasn't enough.

The popular and influential Governor Ed Rendell of Pennsylvania followed Sharpton and bemoaned with a smile, "I'm the guy that was unlucky enough to follow Al Sharpton."

Wayne Barrett Whacks Presidential Candidate Sharpton

Here the ghost of Wayne Barrett (who died in 2017) whispers to us that he, true to form, was still trolling Sharpton in 2004. *The Village Voice* ran one Barrett article after another, with Barrett seeming to feel that in a just world, where newspaper truth-tellers ruled, the villains of the stories should be taken down. Or at least an attempt made.

In a damaging article published on January 27, 2004, Barrett reported that Sharpton's presidential campaign had strong ties to shady Republican strategist Roger Stone. In a deeply researched 4,000-word piece, Barrett revealed that Stone was providing strategic advice and money, including the use of a credit card, to Sharpton as Sharpton was trying to convince Americans he, rather than John Kerry, Howard Dean, or any of the other candidates, would be the best person to represent Democrats against Republican President George W. Bush. Barrett's article was headlined "Sleeping with the GOP." Barrett said Sharpton's ultimate motive was to hurt the Democratic Party because he'd had so many conflicts with it in the past.

Speaking to me in 2020, Sharpton said, "If Barrett's contention was that Roger Stone was using me to hurt the Democrats, here we are fifteen years later: How did I hurt the Democrats? Plus, I ended up being the main campaigner for John Kerry and we are friends to this day . . . ."

Back in 2004, Sharpton told Barrett that he was "sick of these racist double standards" and that well-regarded Democrats had crossed party lines in the past and received assistance from Republicans. He said former President Bill Clinton, for instance, had relied on Republican strategist Dick Morris as an adviser.

Sharpton also told me in 2020 that he'd had a history of working with Stone, who, in the 1990s, as a self-described libertarian, teamed up with progressives and Sharpton's National Action Network to fight the Rockefeller drug laws that were sending so many Blacks to jail.

Sharpton Gets His Way with Trickster Roger Stone

I spoke by phone in the summer of 2020 with the comedian/political strategist who introduced Sharpton to Roger Stone in 2004. That was Randy Credico. Credico was a comedian, radio host, and former political activist with strong ties to white radicals, including the late left-wing attorney William Kunstler. Credico told me that the

Stone–Sharpton relationship was supposed to be mutually beneficial. Sharpton received help and advice from Stone, and Stone was benefiting in the sense that Sharpton's face among the Democratic candidates scared many whites away from the Democratic Party.

"This was a time when Sharpton was toxic to a lot of people. He was considered radical. To some people it was like having Malcolm X . . . . Stone was, I think, looking to sabotage the Democratic Party. He would refer to Sharpton as King Kong whenever he was upset with him."

In the end, Sharpton, ever smooth, with a quick, calculating mind, got more from the relationship than Stone did, Credico said. "I think he used Stone," Credico concluded.

⋮

Things moved along well for a while, Credico said, but then Stone began cutting Credico out of the loop. And so Credico bowed out of the picture, leaving the odd couple to their own devices.

(Credico popped up in the news during Donald Trump's presidency. He had been called to testify against Stone, who had been charged by Special Counsel Robert Mueller with making false statements to Congress, among other alleged wrongdoings. Stone, a longtime confidant of Trump's, was eventually convicted and sentenced to forty months in federal prison. But President Trump commuted the sentence in July 2020, allowing Stone to remain free.)

⋮

Wayne Barrett did not stop with the Roger Stone story in 2004. On November 30, 2004, *The Village Voice* published a Barrett article saying that Sharpton was having a romantic relationship with a female leader of Sharpton's National Action Network. The headline was "On a New High, Sharpton Hits a New Low."

Something needs to be pointed out regarding that Barrett article. No credible mainstream newspaper should have run it. Barrett acknowledged at the beginning of the piece that "[w]hile it is virtually impossible to establish that an intimate relationship existed without confirmation from a party, a compelling case can be made that Sharpton appeared to engage in one with [name withheld] . . . [who had been] named in two *Daily News* gossip pieces."

Sharpton through his lawyers threatened to sue Barrett before the story was published, but the *Voice* went ahead and published it anyway. Sharpton denied there'd been such a relationship.

It was obviously painful for Sharpton. It was around this time that he had announced his separation from his wife of more than twenty years, Kathy Sharpton, the mother of his two daughters, Dominique and Ashley, with whom he was and remains very close. Sharpton has said in the years since that there had not been a divorce and that the couple had an amicable relationship. Sharpton had met Kathy Jordan during his young years traveling with "Godfather of Soul" James Brown, for whom she was a backup singer. (Sharpton in recent years has been open about his new relationship with Aisha McShaw, a fashion designer who is thirty years younger than he.)

Tellingly, and with a touch of humor, Black *Daily News* columnist Errol Louis wrote a follow-up to Barrett's column. The headline was: "The Rev. Houdini: Sharpton's in a Fix Again, but Don't Expect It to Last Long."

The wise and intellectual Louis was right, as he almost always is. The "fix" did not last long. Sharpton began to climb further up the ladder of national attention and influence as the years went by. Sharpton continued working the political circuit and stoking his ties to powerful members of Congress, such as the influential South Carolina Congressman James Clyburn, who through the 2000s was the third-ranking Democratic member of Congress, behind Speaker Nancy Pelosi, who became House Speaker (for the second time) in 2019, and Steny Hoyer, who became Majority Leader that year. Through

President Barack Obama's years in the White House, Sharpton emerged as an alter ego for him in the nation's Black communities. Sharpton also began venturing into talk-show hosting as he continued to speak regularly to listeners on popular radio stations and eventually acquired a position as host of the MSNBC cable news program *PoliticsNation*.

A new communications order was being established. And Rev. Al was climbing to its heights.

Last-minute note: In mid-February 2021, Rev. Sharpton filed for divorce from Kathy Jordan Sharpton, after more than four decades of marriage. In a text message exchange, Sharpton told me that Katherine agreed to sign the papers also. Asked if he planned to marry his much younger girlfriend, Aisha McShaw, he replied, "No comment on that. Premature to even discuss."

10

:::

A New Day, a New Journalism, a King Emerges

NEW YORK NEWSDAY could be called the newspaper that put Al Sharpton on the stage of controversy in the 1980s. With its FBI and Tawana Brawley stories, it wrote Acts 4 and 5 of the Sharpton tragi-comedy.

New York Newsday was at its heights then and into the '90s, with Pulitzer Prizes and metropolitan reporting that was amphetamine for the warring newspapers of New York City. "On top of the news, ahead of the times," *New York Newsday* swanked in its ads. It was positioning itself against the *Daily News*, the almost century-old tabloid of the people (i.e., ethnic whites), and the staid, uppity *New York Times*, which seemed to care more about Beirut than the "outer boroughs" of New York City.

It all came to a crashing halt on July 14, 1995. That was the day the owners of *Newsday* announced they were closing its New York City edition.

The reporters, photographers, editors, and news assistants were crushed. The optimism they'd harbored for journalism took a blow to the gut. Intensifying the fury was that the final decision on whether *New York Newsday* would survive had been made by Mark H. Willes. Willes was the chairman and chief executive officer of *Newsday*'s owner, the Times Mirror Company. He had previously been a top executive with General Mills, the maker of breakfast foods. Journalists in New York City and beyond began labeling him the "Cereal Killer."

In July 2020, Steve Isenberg, who had been the publisher of *New York Newsday* at the time of its shutdown in July 1995, shared remembrances of that place and time. He did so on the Facebook page of the old "Newsday Family." Isenberg, at that moment, the twenty-fifth anniversary of the paper's closing, wanted to let the old crew know he still loved them. He wrote that he was hurt that the Covid-19 shutdown had dashed hopes of reuniting in the flesh.

"In our younger days, we were part of an ambitious enterprise to cover the life of New York City, its people, institutions and pulse with vitality and verve," wrote Isbenberg, who turned eighty in 2020. "In that era of ink on paper, all hands within the paper's operations, in printing, distribution, sales, promotion and community affairs, were partners in our adventure."

Isenberg's résumé reveals something of the character of journalism as it was trying to develop in the latter half of the twentieth century. He earned a bachelor's in English from the University of California, a master's in English literature from Worcester, Oxford, and a Doctor of Law degree from Yale Law School. After *New York Newsday* crashed, Isenberg became interim president and then chair of Adelphi University, and then executive director of the PEN American Center, the U.S. division of the world's oldest literary and human rights organization.

Among *New York Newsday* reporters who stood out in Isenberg's memory was Jim Dwyer. Isenberg chatted with me over the phone about Dwyer, about how other newspapers were trying to hire him away from *New York Newsday*. Isenberg didn't recall what the final salary offer was for keeping Dwyer, but *New York Newsday* reporters appreciated by their bosses were earning six-figures in the '90s, a damn good salary. *New York Newsday* sports columnist Mike Lupica was said to be making more than $500,000 a year.

Neither Isenberg nor I knew it as we spoke of Dwyer then, but Dwyer was soon to succumb from complications of lung cancer. Immediately upon his death on October 8, 2020, at the age of sixty-three, he was hailed in newspapers and broadcast networks around the country as one of the great journalists of the past half-century. He had spent the past nineteen years writing for the *New York Times.*

Like so many other reporters, Dwyer was Irish American and Catholic. He had graduated from Loyola High School in Manhattan and then from Fordham University, where he had discovered his calling to the craft of journalism at the student newspaper, *The Fordham Ram.*

Dwyer was known for his kindness, but he could be bold and blunt when writing about public figures. Al Sharpton was surely a public figure.

In 2014, Dwyer expressed concerns about Sharpton's relationship with Sanford Rubenstein. Rubenstein was a lawyer who had long been associated with Sharpton as Sharpton spoke out for families of Black men killed by police. Rubenstein in the 1990s had been almost exclusively a personal-injury attorney. Then he came into wide public view with the 1997 Abner Louima case in Brooklyn. A cop had shoved a baton up Louima's anus. Rubenstein represented Louima in court filings about the case. Over the next two decades, Rubenstein would represent one police-brutality victim after another, with Sharpton at his side.

A perception problem was that Rubenstein could come off as a huckster and ambulance chaser. In commercials, he tells listeners that victims of police brutality may be entitled to compensation for their suffering. Which is true. And it's also true that much of the money they receive would go to him (and his law partner, Scott Rynecki).

In October 2014, Rubenstein drew media attention again, but this time after an accusation that he had sexually assaulted a woman who happened to have been a leader in Al Sharpton's National Action Network. (The assault allegedly occurred in Rubenstein's penthouse after he, the woman, and others had left a fête celebrating Sharpton's sixtieth birthday.) Sharpton announced that, while he did not know details about the accusation, he was ending his long relationship with Rubenstein. And Dwyer the reporter asked what many considered a sensible question:

"Won't rupturing ties with Mr. Rubenstein cost the National Action Network in financial support?"

Sharpton told Dwyer, as he recently told me, that Rubenstein did not give money to him or to the National Action Network.

In 2016 Manhattan District Attorney Cyrus Vance Jr.'s office said he would not file charges in the accusations against Rubenstein. A year later city newspapers reported that the accuser had dropped her civil suit. But Rubenstein would continue to represent minorities filing multi-million-dollar lawsuits against the police department, all through the decade.

⁞⁞⁞

Last, concerning Dwyer, he stood out among white reporters for the credibility of the remorse he expressed after the 2002 revelations that five convicted Black and Latino men had not actually committed the rape of the white "Central Park jogger." The vigor of the coverage by white newspapers led to the tough prosecution and sentencing of the young men, critics said. (See Chapter 4 on the gender-based racism of the media.) In one of his very last columns with the *Times*, on

May 30, 2019, Dwyer wrote: "Fallibility runs in the human blood-
line, and people from many quarters of public life had not done their
jobs well, including journalists like me."

In 2012 he had been one of the voices in a Ken Burns documentary about the tragedy, "The Central Park Five." And in 2014, Dwyer
wrote a book titled *False Conviction: Innocence, Guilt, and Science.*
Published by Touch Press, it looked into experiences of people
punished for crimes they had not committed. It was done with the
assistance of the Innocence Project and the New York Hall of
Science.

The New Realm

Jim Dwyer and his cohort came from a time forgotten, when white
newspapers ruled the realm. They proclaimed themselves protectors
of the people, doing what they did without fear or favor. They had no
fear of being shouted down in their pursuits, because they always
had the last word.

This all changed . . .

The obliteration of American newspapers continued through the
decades of the new century. In 2020, during the Covid-19 pandemic,
the *New York Daily News*, once romanticized in movies as the model
of old-fashioned, trusted journalism, shut down its remaining office,
in Manhattan. With its staff already having been reduced to a slim
skeleton of its old self, some wondered if the *News* would soon cease
publishing. In the year of the pandemic, Columbia Global Reports
published a book that said it all. It was *Ghosting the News: Local
Journalism and the Crisis of American Democracy*, by Margaret
Sullivan, who noted that more than 2,000 American newspapers had
gone out of business since 2004 and that some cities and towns had

become "news deserts," with no local newspapers at all. Sullivan had once been editor of the *Buffalo News* in upstate New York and went on to serve three years as the "public editor" of the *New York Times*. She is currently a columnist with the *Washington Post*.

Al Sharpton at the Top

As *New York Newsday* announced its closing in July 1995, columnist Sheryl McCarthy reflected on the new world that journalists were entering. Referring to the craft of reporting, she said, "It's not quite the same as becoming a minister, yet it is a kind of calling." (That was in a *New York Times* article of July 23, 1995, "Advice to a Newspaper Dreamer," by Robin Pogrebin.)

As it happened, there was in fact a minister who would soon step into the new media universe and occupy perches once claimed exclusively by Golden Age journalists.

Sharpton began entering the media realm at that moment, in the mid-1990s, as many of its old practitioners were departing. The skill that took him along the path was not old-fashioned reporting and writing but rather the art of speaking with vigor and effect into microphones of radio stations. Back in the 1990s, WLIB was the station that mattered to Blacks wanting to be informed or fired up. WLIB was owned then by Percy Sutton, the late Harlem politician and entrepreneur (though it changed ownership over the coming decade). Sutton, and his buddy/ally Al Sharpton, could see the writing on the wall. The Internet and cable television would soon be more meaningful to journalism than newspapers, in terms of impact and news jobs available. Even before the turning of the century, Sutton obtained licensing to own and operate the Queens Inner Unity Cable Television Systems. And Sharpton would soon be making his own foray into cable, as a paid host.

In April 2020, the Pew Research Center noted that while the number of newspaper newsroom employees had dropped by 51 percent between 2008 and 2019—from about 71,000 workers to 35,000—the reverse was happening with non-print forms of media. "Combined newsroom employment in the other four news-producing industries—broadcast television, radio, cable and digital-native—remained relatively stable, even rising modestly after 2014. Between 2008 and 2014, the number of newsroom employees averaged about 43,000, increasing to about 53,000 by 2019," reported the Pew Center.

Television began to seem like a natural fit for Rev. Al Sharpton. In his splendid suits and ties, with tightly slicked-back hair, he appears on a television screen to be standing and sitting where he always wanted to be. In the old days, he would often garble phrases, even as he never halted the flow of words. He would boom with vigor and confidence even as some began to poke fun, for example, at his mispronunciations. He became a master craftsman, especially regarding his own development.

In 2011, Sharpton became the host of MSNBC's *PoliticsNation* and remained with the cable network through the decade. Tough and determined, he survived complaints that he had gained favor with Comcast, the station's owner, by vocally supporting Comcast as it sought approval from the Federal Communications Commission for a license. It was clear to veteran reporters that the virtues they had long embraced were fading. The old vows to avoid conflicts of interest, even the appearances of them, were no longer required in the new media world, a world in which cable news was ascending. "Rarely, if ever, has a cable news channel employed a host who has previously campaigned for the business goals of the channel's parent company," declared the *New York Times* in a July 27, 2011, article by Brian Stelter about Sharpton and Comcast. "But as channels like MSNBC have moved to more opinionated formats, they have exposed themselves to potential conflicts."

Regarding Sharpton, a clear further conflict was that he was effectively a national political figure and his expected hiring at MSNBC could—would—empower his National Action Network and strengthen his credibility as the nation's "civil rights activist," with backroom clout that rivaled the "pull" of executives of big banks.

Some members of the National Association of Black Journalists complained that Comcast was not truly showing commitment to diversity in giving Sharpton a program. They said Comcast should be offering more opportunities to trained journalists.

###

Sharpton, without a college degree, kept stepping upward in the pecking order of the media elite. In his recent book, *Rise Up*, Sharpton makes clear that his social sphere includes those under the new label of progressive. They are not just Blacks, but also gays, Latinos, Asians, and all struggling immigrants. It's as if he's seeing the direction of the Democratic Party and is set on being part of its leadership, even as he interviews its U.S. senators, congressmembers, and local elected officials. (He insists, to this day, that he has no intention of running for elective office himself.)

Sharpton's media perch does not rest only on his position with MSNBC. For many years he's also hosted programs on radio stations across the country. He does so through the Urban One/Radio One network, a chain of dozens of stations owned and founded by the super-wealthy entrepreneur Cathy Hughes. In the 1980s, in Washington, D.C., Hughes confronted white journalism, in something of the way Sharpton did, though without Tawana Brawley–type distractions. In 1986 she led three months of protests against the *Washington Post*, saying the paper showed patterns of racism in its coverage of Blacks. She continued to acquire stations over the decades. Her Radio One is a publicly traded company.

###

Inextricably woven into his media life is Sharpton's life as a political influencer. It was in 1991, after his stabbing in Bensonhurst, that Sharpton established the National Action Network. NAN set up shop initially on Bedford Avenue in Bedford-Stuyvesant, Brooklyn, and then, after 1995, moved to successive locations in Harlem, now at 145th Street and Malcolm X Boulevard, where it hopes to begin building a permanent House of Justice headquarters with a public auditorium for rallies as well as what it is calling a "library of activism."

NAN has become the heart of Sharpton's clout within the Democratic Party in the twenty-first century. It has scores of chapters through the Northeast, the South, the Midwest, the West, and Gulf regions. Its activities are shared in video clips on its website and at local meetings involving activists and politicians. Sharpton often sleeps just several hours a night, a restless pattern that goes back to his young adulthood. He is continually on the move, traveling around the country through a given week, for meetings and speaking engagements. And, from time to time, too many times, sadly, there are the eulogies that put the nation back in touch with its horrid history of shooting and killing unarmed Black men.

Having never acquired a driver's license, Sharpton is chauffeured everywhere he goes locally, from his Manhattan offices at MSNBC or NAN or his luxury apartment on the Upper East Side. (He moves about with security, he says, given threats against him.)

As for the future of *PoliticsNation*, Sharpton says it's OK. In 2019 he signed a contract to stay with MSNBC for three more years. Civil rights, he says, will be his work forever.

11

###

Confessions of a Hack
(i.e., Old-time Tabloid Reporter)

UNTIL A FEW years ago, I was not so impressed with the "new" Al Sharpton. Even as the Rev. was winning the hearts and minds of so many Black Americans, I harbored distrust that lingered from my younger reporting days. The suspicions largely had to do with my assuming he had indeed been trying to help the FBI capture fugitive Black revolutionary Assata Shakur in the 1980s—and was denying it.

Assata is a legend and folk heroine to so many Blacks. It's not because they delight in the 1973 shooting death of New Jersey State Trooper Werner Foerster, whom Assata was convicted of killing. It's because she became a symbol of resistance to the violence that Blacks had been subjected to for centuries in America. And her 1979 escape from prison made her story all the more awesome to Blacks accustomed to assassinations of Black leaders in the 1960s.

Despite Sharpton's denials, I wrote newspaper articles reporting that he was indeed doing the bidding of federal law enforcement back in the '80s. In the *Daily News* of April 13, 2014, I had an article headlined "Sharpton and His Bugged Briefcase." It quoted a couple of 1980s Black activists who said Sharpton had been trying to get them to tell what they knew about Assata. One of the activists,

Kwame Brathwaite, said Sharpton had told him that he (Sharpton) knew people who would give Assata $50,000 to help her while she was underground. Brathwaite in turn reached out to Black revolutionary Ahmed Obafemi, who agreed to meet with Sharpton and did. But Obafemi ended contact with Sharpton after feeling uneasy about the minister. Speaking to me for that article, Obafemi said he was convinced that Sharpton had recording devices in the suitcases he carried around with him. A few months after that *Daily News* article, on August 25, 2014, I wrote an article for the QZ website with the headline "The Media Need Al Sharpton More Than Black America Does." (QZ was owned by Atlantic Media, publisher of *The Atlantic* magazine.)

What changed between me and Rev. Al?

A few years ago I found myself anxious as I was fighting workplace battles familiar to too many Black professionals. I came to believe that I needed to adjust some of my rooted patterns of behavior in order to survive and be an example for those I loved. Something in me began to appreciate the boldness of Sharpton's verbal bullets aimed on air at Donald J. Trump.

And then I read a story in the *New York Daily News* that gripped me. The December 4, 2017, article ("Brooklyn Contractor Ponies up $625G in Lawsuit Claiming Workers Subjected to Racial Slurs, Segregation," by Greg B. Smith) contained fewer than 600 words. But it unsettled me greatly.

Laquila, a Brooklyn-based contractor, had been found by the EEOC (U.S. Equal Employment Opportunity Commission) to have discriminated against its Black laborers in the most offensive of ways. White foremen had called Black laborers who wore dreadlocks "mop heads." Maybe worst of all, the white "superiors" had set up separate outdoor bathrooms for Blacks. I was born and raised in Brooklyn, New York, as were my parents, and I couldn't recall another case so blatantly like pre–civil rights racist Mississippi.

I never saw any follow-up to the story. I couldn't find articles in any other papers.

I called at least half a dozen Black elected officials to get a comment, thinking it was a no-brainer for a Black politician to be outraged by such activity and demonstrate and demand further punishment. To my dismay, I couldn't get reactions. No one was willing. And when I called Laquila, explaining I wanted to talk to someone about the matter, the lady answering the phone just hung up on me.

Finally, I called Rev. Al. I took some solace in the astonishment and anger I heard in his voice. I wrote a post about the matter on my BrooklynRon website, with a headline quoting Sharpton as saying, of the elected officials, "They must be compromised." This made some sense, since Laquila had operated with local government contracts; and a search of news clippings showed past mob ties.

Sharpton sent his National Action Network's crisis director, Rev. Kevin McCall, to meet with me at Laquila's headquarters, which takes up several blocks in the heavily Caribbean East Flatbush section of Brooklyn. Rev. McCall tried to get someone to answer the front door, but we were not welcome. We parted and said we'd stay in touch.

Overwhelmed with teaching demands and a book I was working on, I retreated. I saw no further public pressure applied to Laquila. But I appreciated what Sharpton had done.

In researching this book, it became clear to me how smooth Rev. Al can be when it comes to making good with journalists who had once bashed him in print. (Note to readers: Regarding the names of Black politicians whom I could not get to publicly criticize the discriminatory policies of Laquila, if someone convinced me they had need for some of the names, I would talk. My concern is that I did not pursue those officials with the persistence I would have applied if I had been working for a news outlet. That said, I still believe all Black elected officials from Brooklyn should have come out with strong public declarations after that *Daily News* article on Laquila. The silence was, and is, heartbreaking.)

Apart from Laquila, something else happened to me in that time frame *vis-à-vis* my thinking about Rev. Al. As I read about him on the web over the past few years, I began experiencing irritation when I saw postings strongly attacking him for his anti-Semitism of the 1990s. For sure, Sharpton could be stupidly crude when speaking of people he didn't like at that moment, and the words could be especially vilifying if he knew the comment could be quoted in some publication. Let's not forget the tongue-lashings he and Alton Maddox gave to so many "Uncle Tom" Black politicians who expressed any disagreement with them.

If you've been listening to Sharpton on cable television and reading his books in recent years, you may agree with me on this: His politesse, whether it has to do with Jews or gays, is at the highest reaches of PC. He will stress the strong role of Jews in the civil rights movement, and he'll mention his gay sister and diligently refer to a Latino person as a Latinx.

But it's clear that Crown Heights became a sticking stain on the Rev., in the minds of many Jews (and others, especially right-wingers who use the anti-Semite tag as a convenient political trope).

Two years ago, after my book *Boss of Black Brooklyn: The Life and Times of Bertram L. Baker* came out, I was looking to do launches. Park Slope Community Bookstore seemed like a fitting locale. I'd known Ezra Goldstein, one of the owners, for years, and he liked the idea of my having something at his place. Ezra's only stipulation was that we should have a big-name person as co-host, to ask me questions and toss out thoughts of their own. I eventually thought to myself, who around town is a bigger name than Al Sharpton? Having no idea what his response would be, I asked Rev. and he said yes right away. But to my utter dismay, Ezra said they couldn't do something like that with Al Sharpton, because the store had to be sensitive to the feelings of its customers. They were largely Jewish, he said, and they remained strongly resentful of Al Sharpton's "anti-Semitic" comments and actions in the past. Presumably, the anger had to do largely with the 1991 Crown Heights riots. (That conflict between Blacks and Hasidic Jews in Central Brooklyn is recounted in Chapter 8, "'I Know Jews from Italians.'")

A publicity person I was working with asked if I'd consider partnering with someone else, in light of the Community Bookstore's concerns. But there's no way I could have felt comfortable with myself if I had done that. And so, I dropped any plans to promote *Boss of Black Brooklyn* at the Community Bookstore. Last, regarding the Rev.'s anti-Semitic comments, I thought I had more right to be upset with him for the things he'd done, say—OK, allegedly—regarding Assata Shakur.

I decided forty-five years ago to enter "the craft" of journalism, because I wasn't sure I could do anything else to earn a living. I knew how to write sentences in understandable English. Especially appealing was that I didn't have to worry about being sharply dressed or speaking like an actor or a lawyer. I was shy. In the craft all you had to do was ask simple questions, take notes, and then write the quick story.

I used to tell my journalism students that being a journalist was like taking religious vows: to be transparent, to seek and find the truth, to report it without fear or favor. But back in the Golden Age, we were guilty of a grave sin: We caved to the lure of loud headlines, mindlessly chasing the same stories, like birds on a wire. And it was this more than anything else that led to the naissance of the Al Sharpton that so many came to dislike and others more recently to love.

Though I had written about Rev. Al over the years, he was never a beat of mine. As Michael Klein said of me thirty years ago in his authorized biography of Sharpton, *The Man Behind the Sound Bite: The Real Story of the Rev. Al Sharpton*, I was a Black guy who did Black stories from time to time, popping in and popping out.

I actually liked writing about communities and people I didn't know well.

In 1983 I went to take summer graduate courses at Iberoamericana, a Jesuit university in Mexico City. I could sense the changes taking place in New York City. I wanted to be more comfortable with the Latino communities that were just starting to be visible in New York. After my summer courses in Mexico, I went knocking on doors looking for work. I went to the offices of the Associated Press in Mexico City. Peter Eisner, the AP's News Editor for Mexico and Central America, welcomed me into his office, chatted with me, and said, "Sure, we'll hire you." I almost fainted. Over two years, I reported stories out of Mexico, Nicaragua, and El Salvador.

Peter is a model old-school journalist. I admired his honesty, his commitment to friends and family, his love of truth-seeking and -telling, his decency. I remember, when I was into my first week or so at the AP in Mexico City, one of the Mexican writers was talking on a landline about ten feet from me, pleasantly telling someone, in Spanish, that they had a new reporter, a "Negrito," in the office. Almost on cue, I heard Peter's voice from the distance, saying, "_____, necisitamos hablar en la oficina—ahora." ("_____, we need to speak in my office, right now.") We never talked about it, but I had little doubt he was telling the writer that the word *Negrito* was not to be used again, in the office, to describe me. And it never was.

When not in the AP office writing or outside reporting, I developed friendships with Mexicans. We would sometimes travel together with our respective families. (My wife, Marilyn, a law school graduate, had a job with a law firm that needed an English speaker. Our son Damani was in grammar school and becoming very comfortable with Spanish.) When I was with my Mexican buddies, we would have our guitars with us and play and sing Mexican ranchera songs.

Journalists are restless people. Peter left and went to *Newsday*, where he became Foreign Editor, based in Suffolk County, Long Island. Within a year, in late 1984, I also was hired by *Newsday*, returning to my hometown of New York City. As if someone above were guiding and looking out for us, Peter became best of friends with *Newsday* Assistant Managing Editor Les Payne, and Les Payne became a mentor to me.

It was Peter who worked with Les as Les took on the Tawana Brawley story. After Les's sudden death in 2018, Peter and I talked and he said, "Why not do a book on Al Sharpton?" My first reaction was, What? He thought Sharpton was one of the most interesting of the characters we all had dealt with in the fading years of the twentieth century. In late 2019, I decided I'd give it a go. And Fordham University Press seemed to like the idea, to do a story about the Rev. and the white newspapers of the late 1900s. A story within a story.

At the turn of the twenty-first century, as so many journalists began running from newsrooms in the emerging new communications environment, Peter also left the trenches. Living in Washington, he has recently been teaching college journalism classes. But more significantly, to me and Les Payne, Peter began writing one significant book after another. Peter is, in many ways, emblematic of the changes that defined post-1960s American reporting. (See in Chapter 7 the references to Bob Woodward, Carl Bernstein, and the "New Journalism.")

Peter wrote or co-wrote these books in the twenty-first century, after he had put his news career behind him:

> *High Crimes: The Corruption, Impunity, and Impeachment of Donald Trump*, Peter Eisner and Michael D'Antonio, Thomas Dunne Books, 2020.
> *Cuba Libre: A 500-Year Quest for Independence*, Peter Eisner and Philip Brenner, Rowman & Littlefield, 2018.
> *The Shadow President: The Truth about Mike Pence*, Peter Eisner and Michael D'Antonio, Thomas Dunne Books, 2018.

MacArthur's Spies: The Soldier, the Singer, and the Spymaster Who Defied the Japanese in World War II, Peter Eisner, Penguin Books, 2017.

The Pope's Last Crusade: How an American Jesuit Helped Pope Pius XI's Campaign to Stop Hitler, Peter Eisner, William Morrow, 2013.

The Italian Letter: How the Bush Administration Used a Fake Letter to Build the Case for War in Iraq, Peter Eisner and Knut Royce, Rodale, 2007.

The Freedom Line: The Brave Men and Women Who Rescued Allied Airmen from the Nazis During World War II, Peter Eisner, William Morrow, 2004.

At Les Payne's seventy-fifth-birthday celebration, held at the Williamsburg, Brooklyn, site of the Brooklyn Brewery, I made a comment in the open forum at which each attendee offered a thought about Les, what he had meant to them as journalists. Most of us were long gone from *Newsday*. Hosting the "open mic" was Peter, his very close colleague and friend.

I remember saying that Les and Peter were, for me, the formation of a circle. Together they made me what I became as a journalist. They were the matchmakers between me and Cuba, where I met and interviewed Assata Shakur; where I roamed the island writing about musicians and everyday citizens; where I interviewed Fidel Castro in the Presidential Palace; where, in more recent years, I took Stony Brook University journalism students to learn about that storied isle.

History is always with us. It was Fidel Castro who, back in 1984, had granted Assata asylum, allowing her to live in Cuba. After her 1979 escape from prison, she was believed, for at least a stretch of time, to have been holed up in the Bedford-Stuyvesant section of Brooklyn. That's likely why the FBI wanted Sharpton to become involved in locating her, I've concluded.

Interestingly, on January 2, 2021, the *New York Post* ran a story (page 10) reporting that the FBI is making "renewed calls for help in tracking down one of the most wanted terrorists (JoAnne Chesimard) .... The FBI is offering $1 million for any tips that directly lead to her arrest." Who knows now how that saga will end?

But this I do know: that Assata and Cuba were together the seed of this book.

Special thanks to Peter Eisner, Les Payne, and, yes, Rev. Al.

ACKNOWLEDGMENTS

IN THE FIRST sentence of this book's Introduction, I mentioned 2020 as being the year of America's reckoning with race *and* a raging virus. Death always seemed so close by. Many everyday Americans shut their social lives totally down.

But if there were no other benefits from that novel virus, it helped many of us who are introspective come to some terms with the meaning of life. I and others, with measures of guilt, believed the confinement was offering tangible benefits. I recall a smug empathy as I read a *New York Times* article written in the first weeks of the shutdown. It was headlined: "'I Like It, Actually'—Why So Many Older People Thrive in Lockdown." It ran on April 24, 2020.

Researching and writing this book in less than a year, as per an agreement with Brooklyn College, where I teach composition and journalism, and Fordham University Press, seemed horribly daunting at first. But I was able to do it without crashing in agony because of my forced existence in the cave of the shutdown. I spent many hundreds of hours exploring library databases of old articles and journals, as well as using apps that allowed me to record phone interviews and have them transcribed. And then there was the writing.

To Whom I Owe It All

My live-in companion through it all was Marilyn Henry Howell. Fifty years ago, in 1971, I was asked a question by Judge William Booth, the late New York Supreme Court Justice/radical civil rights attorney. Would I be with Marilyn "for better for worse, for richer, for poorer, in sickness and in health, to love and to cherish" until my end? I answered that I would. Marilyn, too, responded in the affirmative when she was asked.

Marilyn is so much tougher than I am. Several decades ago, she battled a life-threatening illness and then went on to a career as an attorney in New York State's Family Court system. Her loving generosity leaves me speechless. Over the years, even though she would have preferred to stay in our hometown of Brooklyn, she bounced around with me, this vagabond journalist, as I honed my craft in Michigan, Maryland, and Mexico. Marilyn says I chose those places because I love M's. There must be something to that. Our physician son Damani's three children call Marilyn their Mommy M.

Now retired, Marilyn loves fiction and reads all the time. I rarely identify as a writer, choosing reporter or journalist as my label. It's been a blessing for me that Marilyn—the fiction lover who does beautiful paintings—has graciously served as my editor/proofreader as I've worked on long articles or books over the years. On this book, *King Al*, she was indispensable.

Through the surges in the pandemic in New York, Marilyn and I hunkered down, and we grew in our love for each other. It was a coming together of body and soul that no vacation had ever bequeathed us.

TOOLS THAT MADE THE BOOK

OVER APPROXIMATELY A year, I interviewed scores of journalists, activists, politicians, and others who were familiar with New York City when it was a marching ground for the Rev. Al Sharpton. This time frame covered the last four decades of the twentieth century. Rev. Al, generously, spoke with me for hours and exchanged text messages. Interviews were mostly conducted by phone, given that work was largely done during New York City's Covid-19 shutdown.

Good journalism almost always involves history. This journalist submerged himself in rich archival databases of newspapers, magazines, and scholarly journals. One of the keys was ProQuest, the content/technology company that stores articles, dissertations, academic journals, and magazines dating back decades. I spent more than a thousand hours searching for and reading old articles from the *New York Amsterdam News*, the *New York Daily News*, the *New York Times*, *Newsday*, the *New York Post*, *The Village Voice*, and *The New Yorker*, among others.

Particularly helpful to me as I researched were librarians, including Sheena Philogene at Brooklyn College; librarians at the Brooklyn Public Library and the New York Public Library; and librarians at two New York City daily newspapers who aided me as a personal

153

favor throughout my research. Most notable and gracious in that last category was Laura Mann of *Newsday*.

To develop a feel for times past, it was helpful to hear and see scenes from the 1960s and following decades. The Vanderbilt Television News Archive was a valuable resource. Relevant documentaries were found via YouTube Premium, Vimeo, and Netflix.

Though it's not on the following list of books, I read the Bible, paying special attention to the New Testament, the foundation of Black Christianity. Worthy of mention is that two of the four books about Rev. Sharpton were written in collaboration with two gifted Black "Golden Age" writers, one being Nick Chiles, who once reported for *Newsday*, the other being Karen Hunter, who, among other achievements at the *Daily News*, won a Pulitzer Prize.

Rise Up: Confronting a Country at the Crossroads, by Al Sharpton, Hanover Square Press, 2020.

Reverend Al Sharpton: The Rejected Stone, by Reverend Al Sharpton with Nick Chiles, Cash Money Content (Massenburg Media), 2013.

Al on America, by Reverend Al Sharpton, with Karen Hunter, Dafina Books–Kensington Publishing Corp., 2002.

Go and Tell Pharaoh: The Autobiography of the Reverend Al Sharpton, by Al Sharpton and Anthony Walton, Doubleday, 1996.

The Man Behind the Sound Bite: The Real Story of the Rev. Al Sharpton, by Michael Klein, Castillo International, 1991.

Black Religious Intellectuals: The Fight for Equality from Jim Crow to the 21st Century, by Clarence Taylor, Routledge, Taylor & Francis Group, 2002.

The Black Churches of Brooklyn, by Clarence Taylor, Columbia University Press, 1994.

Within the Veil: Black Journalists, White Media, by Pamela Newkirk, New York University Press, 2000.

The Life of Kings: The Baltimore Sun and the Golden Age of the American Newspaper, edited by Frederic B. Hill and Stephens Broening, Rowman & Littlefield, 2016.

Uncovering Race: A Black Journalist's Story of Reporting and Reinvention, by Amy Alexander, Beacon Press, 2011.

News for All the People: The Epic Story of Race and the American Media, by Juan Gonzalez and Joseph Torres, Verso, 2011.

Ghosting the News: Local Journalism and the Crisis of American Democracy, by Margaret Sullivan, Columbia Global Reports/New York, 2020.

City Son: Andrew W. Cooper's Impact on Modern-Day Brooklyn, by Wayne Dawkins, University Press of Mississippi, 2012.

Volunteer Slavery: My Authentic Negro Experience, by Jill Nelson, Penguin Books, 1994.

Why Are the Heroes Always White? by Sheryl McCarthy, Andrews & McMeel, 1995.

No Monopoly on Suffering: Blacks and Jews in Crown Heights and Elsewhere, by Herbert D. Daughtry, Africa World Press, 1997.

The Life and Crimes of Don King: The Shame of Boxing in America, by Jack Newfield, William Morrow, 1995.

African American Religious History: A Documentary Witness, edited by Milton C. Sernett, Duke University Press, 1999.

Jesse Jackson: America's David, by Barbara A. Reynolds, JFK Associates, 1985.

Unholy Alliances: Working the Tawana Brawley Story, by Mike Taibbi and Anna Sims-Phillips, Harcourt Brace Jovanovich, 1989.

Outrage: The Story Behind the Tawana Brawley Hoax, by Robert D. McFadden, Ralph Blumenthal, M. A. Farber, E. R. Shipp, Charles Strum, and Craig Wolff, Bantam Books, 1990.

Black Journalists: The NABJ Story, by Wayne Dawkins, August Press, 1997.

The Campaign: Rudy Giuliani, Ruth Messinger, Al Sharpton, and the Race to Be the Mayor of New York City, by Evan J. Mandery, Westview, 1999.

Black Brooklyn: The Politics of Ethnicity, Class, and Gender, by John Louis Flateau, Ph.D., Author House, 2016.

Kill 'em and Leave: Searching for James Brown and the American Soul, by James McBride, Spiegel and Grau, 2016.

God in the Ghetto, by William A. Jones Jr., Progressive Baptist Publishing House, 1979.

How Shall They Preach, by Gardner C. Taylor, Progressive Baptist Publishing House, 1977.

The Black Church in the African American Experience, by C. Eric Lincoln and Lawrence H. Mamiya, Duke University Press, 1990.

Black Theology & Black Power (20th Anniversary Edition), by James H. Cone, HarperCollins, 1989.

The Sacrifice, by Joyce Carol Oates, HarperCollins, 2015.

Fighting Jim Crow in the County of Kings: The Congress of Racial Equality in Brooklyn, by Brian Purnell, University Press of Kentucky, 2013.

Assata: An Autobiography, by Assata Shakur, Lawrence Hill & Co., 1987.

The Political Biography of an American Dilemma: Adam Clayton Powell, Jr., by Charles V. Hamilton, Atheneum, 1991.

Adam by Adam: The Autobiography of Adam Clayton Powell, Jr., by Adam Clayton Powell Jr., The Dial Press, 1971.

Adam Clayton Powell: Portrait of a Marching Black, by James Haskins, The Dial Press, 1974.

Rudy: An Investigative Biography of Rudolph Giuliani, by Wayne Barrett, Basic Books, 2000.

Trump: The Greatest Show on Earth: The Deals, the Downfall, the Reinvention, by Wayne Barrett, Regan Arts, 2016. (Originally published as *Trump: The Deals and the Downfall*, HarperCollins, 1992.)

Without Compromise: The Brave Journalism That First Exposed Donald Trump, Rudy Giuliani, and the American Epidemic of Corruption, by Wayne Barrett (ed. Eileen Markey), Bold Type Press, 2020.

America's Last Great Newspaper War: The Death of Print in a Two-Tabloid Town, by Mike Jaccarino, Fordham University Press, 2020.

The Bonfire of the Vanities, by Tom Wolfe, Picador–Farrar, Straus & Giroux, 1987.

Newsday: A Candid History of the Respectable Tabloid, by Robert F. Keeler, Arbor House/William Morrow, 1990.

Scoop, by Evelyn Waugh, Penguin Books, 2003 (first published in 1938).

Why Blacks Fear America's Mayor: Reporting Police Brutality and Black Activist Politics Under Rudy Giuliani, by Peter Noel, iUniverse, 2007.

Liberal Racism, by Jim Sleeper, Rowman & Littlefield, 2002.

Closest of Strangers: Liberalism and the Politics of Race in New York, by Jim Sleeper, Norton, 1990.

The Jesus Bag, by William H. Grier, M.D., and Price M. Cobbs, M.D., McGraw-Hill, 1971.

A Black Theology of Liberation, by James H. Cone, Orbis Books, 2010.

Covering America: A Narrative History of a Nation's Journalism, by Christopher B. Daly, University of Massachusetts Press, 2018.

The Dead Are Arising: The Life of Malcolm X, by Les Payne, Liveright Press, 2020.

Savage Portrayals: Race, Media and the Central Park Jogger Story, by Natalie Byfield, Temple University Press, 2014.

Merchants of Truth: The Business of News and the Fight for Facts, by Jill Abramson, Simon & Schuster, 2019.

Upon This Rock: The Miracles of a Black Church, by Samuel G. Freedman, HarperCollins, 1993.

INDEX

Murdoch, Rupert: Facebook and, 5; *New York Post* and, 27
Museum of Civil Rights, Sharpton, Al, and, 14–15

National Action Network (NAN), Sharpton, Al, and, 2–3, 13, 33, 136, 141
National Association of Black Journalists, 21, 25, 140
National Book Foundation, 27
National Youth Movement (NYM), 106; Brown, J., performances for, 87; Brown, T., as member of, 86; financial handling of, 85; Sharpton, Al, and politicians in, 85; Sharpton, Al, misuse of, 87
Nation of Islam, 120–21
Nelson, Jill: Sharpton, Al, and Black politicians denounce Nelson's Mike Tyson protest march, 64
Nelson, Lemrick, 119–20
"newcomers," 71–72
Newfield, Jack, 45, 84, 89–90
Newkirk, Pamela, 24, 62–63
Newsday, Long Island, 20, 22–25, 42; Bethany Baptist Church resentment of, 108; FBI and Sharpton, Al, investigation and, 10–12, 41; Louima story in, 48; Lumumba on Sharpton, Al, in, 6; Payne, L., duties at, 21
News for All the People (González and Torres), 64
Newspaper Guild, 35
newspapers, 117; cable and web news overtaking, 65; death of, 5; job decline at, 66; legendary warning of, 49; obliteration of, 137–38; race-based double standards in, 50, 53; Sharpton, Al, focus in, 20–21; story simplicity in, 70–71; Taylor on Sharpton, Al, and, 115–16; "the wood" in, 36
New York City, Sharpton, Al, lawsuit against, 46
New York City Police Department, 34, 39–40, 50, 117, 119
New York Daily News, 60, 133; author's opinion pieces in, 4; closing of, 137; discrimination suit against, 51; future of,

4–5; Grant murder story and, 61–62; racial double standards at, 53–54; "Sharpton and His Bugged Briefcase" article in, 142–43; "Tell it to Sweeney" saying at, 36–37
New York Newsday, 10, 18, 21; closing of, 133–34; heights of, 133; Isenberg remembrances of, 134; money at, 35–36; Newspaper Guild and, 35; reporter salaries of, 135; Sharpton, Al, FBI dealings article in, 44
New York Post, 5; author on, 4; Covid pandemic and Sharpton, Al, article in, 2–3; Murdoch right-wing approaches in, 27; Sharpton, Al, contrast with Trump, D., in, 4; Sharpton, Al, treatment in, 27; on southern Blacks killings, 27
New York Theological Seminary, 31
New York Times, 5, 60, 133; on Mason and Morgenthau challenge, 30; Payne, L., and Brawley story regarding, 25–26; Wall Street and, 35
Nixon, Richard, 86, 87, 112
Nobile, Philip: Imus campaign of, 29–30; Sharpton, Al, Brawley story interview of, 28–29
Noel, Peter, Stewart, M., case coverage by, 33–34
NYM. *See* National Youth Movement

Obafemi, Ahmed, 12; on Sharpton, Al, 42–43; on Sharpton, Al, and recording devices, 143
Obama, Barack, Sharpton, Al, and, 12, 14, 16, 132
Operation Breadbasket, 101
Orbison, Roy, 28
Owens, Chris (son), 80; education of, 81; hero of, 82; on Sharpton, Al, and father, 81–82
Owens, Ethel Werfel (wife), 73
Owens, Major, 75, 77, 78, 80–81; Barrett collaboration with, 73–74; Blacks view of, 83; Sharpton, Al, election episode with, 73–74; Sharpton, Al, *Newsday* article on, 42; Sharpton, Al, secret phone recording of, 74; Stewart, W., on, 83

Ron Howell is a journalist/teacher. He is currently an Associate Professor in the English Department at Brooklyn College. In 2019, Fordham University Press published his biography of his maternal grandfather, *Boss of Black Brooklyn: The Life and Times of Bertram L. Baker.* In past decades, Howell was a full-time reporter/writer, successively, with the *Baltimore Evening Sun, Ebony* magazine, the *New York Daily News, The Associated Press* (in Mexico), and *Newsday.*

EMPIRE
STATE
EDITIONS   SELECT TITLES FROM EMPIRE STATE EDITIONS

Susan Celia Greenfield (ed.), *Sacred Shelter: Thirteen Journeys of Homelessness and Healing*

Elizabeth Macaulay-Lewis and Matthew M. McGowan (eds.), *Classical New York: Discovering Greece and Rome in Gotham*

Susan Opotow and Zachary Baron Shemtob (eds.), *New York after 9/11*

Andrew Feffer, *Bad Faith: Teachers, Liberalism, and the Origins of McCarthyism*

Colin Davey with Thomas A. Lesser, *The American Museum of Natural History and How It Got That Way*. Forewords by Neil deGrasse Tyson and Kermit Roosevelt III

Wendy Jean Katz, *Humbug: The Politics of Art Criticism in New York City's Penny Press*

Lolita Buckner Inniss, *The Princeton Fugitive Slave: The Trials of James Collins Johnson*

Mike Jaccarino, *America's Last Great Newspaper War: The Death of Print in a Two-Tabloid Town*

Angel Garcia, *The Kingdom Began in Puerto Rico: Neil Connolly's Priesthood in the South Bronx*

Jim Mackin, *Notable New Yorkers of Manhattan's Upper West Side: Bloomingdale–Morningside Heights*

Matthew Spady, *The Neighborhood Manhattan Forgot: Audubon Park and the Families Who Shaped It*

Robert O. Binnewies, *Palisades: 100,000 Acres in 100 Years*

Marilyn S. Greenwald and Yun Li, *Eunice Hunton Carter: A Lifelong Fight for Social Justice*

Jeffrey A. Kroessler, *Planning and Preservation in a Historic Garden Suburb*

Elizabeth Macaulay-Lewis, *Antiquity in Gotham: The Ancient Architecture of New York City*

Phil Rosenzweig, *Reginald Rose and the Journey of "12 Angry Men"*

For a complete list, visit www.fordhampress.com/empire-state-editions.